BRING THE LIGHT TO SCHOOL

How You Can Empower Christian Students From K-12

Ingrid DeDecker

ISBN Paperback: 978-1-7321473-2-4

ISBN EBook: 978-1-7321473-1-7

Libray of Congress Cataloging-in-Publication data is available.

Praise for *BRING THE LIGHT TO SCHOOL*

"*Bring the Light to School* is a well-researched and practically helpful guide for teachers, parents, pastors, youth workers, and anyone God is calling to impact our public schools—the most strategic mission field in our nation. This book will answer your questions, even the ones you didn't know you had!"

David Schmus
Executive Director
Christian Educators Association International ceai.org

"*Bring The Light to School* contains invaluable pragmatic advice on Christian student rights. It provides step by step instruction on how to start Christian clubs. Ingrid DeDecker answers the questions about Separation of Church and State as it relates to faith in schools and brings them to a place of clarity and implementation for everyone. In a world of increasing anxiety about the safety and social-emotional wellbeing of our students, this book offers a roadmap to addressing those concerns. It is chock full of legal facts we can use to make a difference instead of cowering under fear-based a much needed assumptions."

Linda McLaughlin
Elementary School Educator, ret.

"*Bring the Light to School* is a much needed book as to how Christian organizers can help Christian students activate Christian clubs to deepen their faith. Our public school heritage has roots with many Christian churches but calls for separation between church and state which led to key Supreme Court decisions such as Engel v. Vitale and Abington School District v. Schempp. These cases disallowed school prayer and scriptures and also centered about the role of religion in public schools. Since these decisions, many Christian organizers needed guidance as to how best to assist students deepen their faith with other like-minded students while attending school. Ingrid DeDecker's book provides much needed guidance and addresses everything from Separation of Church and State to first amendment rights. This book is a must-read.

Dr. Patrick Rice
Author ,*Vanishing School Boards*, former
teacher, principal and adjunct professor

"Ingrid DeDecker identified the most urgent need in our culture — reaching our children for Christ! In her new book, *Bring The Light To School*, she gives practical instructions for how to legally bring the gospel of Jesus to our kids and public schools. We can no longer sit on the sidelines lamenting the fact that God has been taken out of our schools; we now know how to take Him back in! Many thanks to Ingrid for her work in establishing clubs and her research into this need. I pray that Christians will use this information to reach schools in their neighborhoods and communities as well."

Brenda Hedgepeth
Teacher at Brookhaven Academy

"Ingrid DeDecker knows how to connect our kids in public schools. Whether it's in elementary or high school. Her book *Bring the Light to School* is an excellent resource when God calls us to do something for our schools. It shows how to get into public schools and is full of stories and motivation. An excellent book for any parent, pastor, Christian leader or even student."

Jamie Overholt
Senior Leader, Attwell Revival Center

"Bring the Light to School is a thoughtful, comprehensive, well-organized "how to" book to help people share the love of God with students by establishing Christian clubs in public school settings. The book clearly describes First Amendment and equal access rights of students to express their faith in schools as established in court cases. It shows how groups have successfully set up clubs to meet school regulations. It gives insight on how to include school goals such as character education and school curriculum in the club's goals and how to meet public school concerns that schools steer clear of endorsing religion."

"Ingrid DeDecker uses her considerable experience with schools and Christian clubs, as well as her research of many online resources to provide an outline of the considerations and steps needed to set up an effective Christian outreach for student in schools. From gathering volunteers and resources and first approaching the school principal, to providing documents and forms to help invite student and parent participation, to outlining schedules and logistics for setting up a club and conducting successful meetings, Ingrid has included many things that Christian clubs have learned over years of experience that will be useful and necessary for running a club. Detailed footnotes are included that document information for every school level. May the knowledge provided in Bring the Light to School, the love that Ingrid shows for school children and the love of God help you share with your community and make an eternal difference in many lives."

Warren Hershberger,
Public School Teacher, ret.

"Be careful reading this book. It will cause you to believe you can help change a city! I now know how to get a club started that can really make a difference in kid's lives. I was uneducated on First Amendment rights before volunteering with the Torch Club. Ingrid's character education program teaches caring, honesty and responsibility in public schools. Also, having volunteered with the club, I was able to see just how much kids want to learn about God. It's so cool to see how God opens doors so His kids can learn about Him. Kids are our future! This book gives you everything you need to be empowered!"

Mara Broda
Former Torch Club Leader

"As a 43-year teacher veteran, I saw first-hand the importance of the material shared in this very inspiring book. Ingrid DeDecker shares with the reader numerous ideas of how they can implement the teaching of Christian morals, character, leadership and values to our public-school children of all ages, legally. She challenges us to get involved, stop making excuses, and start making a difference in the lives of our young people.

Ingrid answers every possible question that an interested inquirer could possibly have along with much of the needed paper work that will be required. I applaud this author for her insight and professionalism in producing this valuable information."

Mary Thomas,
Math Teacher, ret., #1 Bestselling Author

"Our schools are facing huge challenges. Students are struggling with violence, low self-esteem, bullying and so much more. However, Ingrid Decker has provided a well developed manual for how churches and para church ministries can effectively reach out to their local schools. Her book, *Bring the Light to School*, shows you exactly what you need to know so that your church or ministry can bring hope to the lives of children. I have established a Christian club in two public schools with Ingrid's information. I know that it works."

Pastor Samuel Hampton II
The Faith Place, Akron, Ohio

CONTENTS

Documents for Elementary School

PART FOUR High School Clubs

PART FIVE Organizations for Legal Help

PART SIX High School Documents for Principal

PART SEVEN Federal Guidelines On Faith In Schools

Part Eight Appendix

FOREWORD

"All That Is Necessary for Evil to Triumph is for Good Men to do Nothing"

Edmund Burke

We've all grown tired of the news. We are tired of hearing about a secular agenda, gender confusion and Hollywood filth. We are weary of one more story of horrible violence and the consequences of lives not lived God's way.

Yet for too long, well meaning Christians have wrung their hands in despair thinking there are no solutions. We see our children as targets of gay agendas, drug dealers and cruel school peers. They are the object of stalkers, Facebook harassment, sick video games and perverse television shows. Everyone else is targeting our children. Why shouldn't we?

You hold in your hands an awesome and workable solution. It is one that anyone with interest and perseverance can pursue. It is for mothers, grandmothers, fathers. It is for neighbors, teachers, youth leaders and pastors. It is for *you*.

It was written by a woman impassioned to find out what our legal rights really are in the public schools. She is a mother bent on not allowing her children to slip away into the abyss of worldly confusion and seduction.

She succeeded. She discovered we have every right to start Christian clubs in every level of education K-12. She has pioneered the new clubs, in fact in more than a dozen cities in several states.

What does such a club do? It is the antidote for the damaging tide of today. It is a way to reach our children at their most innocent and vulnerable ages and bring God's love into their equation.

It is a consistent way to provide fortresses for these kids in a place of dire need...our schools. It is a way to build fortresses of Christian friendship, strengthened children and well-taught Biblical truths. It is simple, and it is free.

You and I both know that teachers are overloaded today. Society has wrongly shifted the weight of teaching character, social health and family responsibilities where it doesn't belong. Core subjects suffer. The material they are allowed to teach from for these added demands has little meat of virtue or godliness. They are being told to make "bricks without straw," just like the captive Israelites.

We have a solution. We can bring hope. We can bring truth. We can let the "children come to us" as God designed and deliver what is lacking—and it can be fun and creative!
In the pages of this book, you will learn every detail of how to start a Christian club in your school or one near you. As you familiarize yourself with our rights and the process, it will become an easy and delightful quest.

You don't have to do it all yourself. The nature of God and community is shared responsibility. God is rousing His people to step forward and do what is needed to bring sanity back to society and save our kids from destruction. Just look around you and see who you can tap to "catch the vision" with you!

Proverbs 3:27 says, "Do not withhold good from those to whom it is due, when it is in the power of your hand to do it." I say the time is now. We have the answers. The goal is achievable, and the results will be stunning and eternal. Go forth!

Bessie Watson Rhoades
Former personal staff to Senator John Glenn, Ohio
and Senator Barry Goldwater, Arizona
Former professional writer and strategist for the Crisis Pregnancy Centers of Arizona and Major Ministries across the United States

THE NEED

Please look at these statistics about our high schools from the Center for Disease Control[1] for 2015. During the last 12 months

29.9% of students had felt sad or hopeless almost every day for two or more weeks in a row.

17.7% of students had seriously considered attempting suicide

6.7% of students had been physically forced to have sexual intercourse when they did not want to.

19.6% of students had been bullied on school property.

21.9% of students nationwide had ridden one or more times in a car driven by someone who had been drinking alcohol during the 30 days before the survey.

21.7% of students had been offered, sold, or given an illegal drug by someone on school property.

24.3% of students who were sexually active did not use any method to prevent pregnancy during last sexual intercourse.

---

[1] Kann L, Olsen EO, McManus T, et al. Sexual Identity, Sex of Sexual Contacts, and Health-Related Behaviors Among Students in Grades 9–12 — United States and Selected Sites, 2015. MMWR Surveill Summ 2016;65(No. SS-9):1–202. DOI retrievable at:

The MMWR series of publications is published by the Center for Surveillance, Epidemiology, and Laboratory Services, Centers for Disease Control and Prevention (CDC), U.S. Department of Health and Human Services, Atlanta, GA 30329-4027.

7.1% of students had not gone to school on at least 1 day during the 30 days before the survey because they felt they would be unsafe at school or on their way to or from school.

24.7% of students had been in a physical fight.

With this book, I hope for Christians to grasp this amazing opportunity to help our students bypass these terrible statistics. Starting a faith-based character education club or any Christian club will steer our kids toward more hope.

INTRODUCTION

My church had a prayer walk one morning. We could see a school building in front of us. We walked and prayed for this school and I couldn't stop thinking about those students. I knew that God was pointing it out to me. A seed was being planted in my heart to reach those students and tell them how much God loves them.

I was quite comfortable in my international business career, and was sure this nudge from Holy Spirit was something temporary I could just pray about and maybe find out a little more on the side.

But the desire became compelling quickly, and I couldn't shake off the thought. God was arresting me with reminders that He could come through for these kids in their darkest hour just like He had always been there for me- and they needed Him!

I decided to simply contact that first school to see if they had a Christian club. "There, that wasn't so hard," I mused. "What a relief. They already have a Christian club. Maybe God just wants me to keep praying for the kids." This means I could just keep giving money to ministries instead of having to be directly involved, and I could keep my consulting career.

Apparently, God was not as convinced. He put another school nearby on my heart. Again, I couldn't shake off the prompting to see if they had a club. Of course, they didn't. I had rarely heard of such a thing anyway. "Maybe I'll just research a little and find out the truth about the separation of church and state," I concluded.

That is how this story was written. Now, many clubs later in several cities and states, I am seeing God's dream realized and have fully embraced my part in bringing hope to students through leading Partner with Schools. I feel fulfilled in my purpose more than I ever was in setting up subsidiary companies around the world.

My only nudge now is that students need these clubs everywhere if they are to survive the environment of public schools and keep their faith.

You holding this book is an answer to my prayer- and most likely to God's desire, too!

I hope you will be as inspired as I was to take action and make an eternal difference.

I know it will bless you, too!

I have organized this book as a ready reference for each school level. Some information explained earlier in the book might be mentioned again to make sure it is included in its category. This way you have it all together when needed.

PART ONE

Student Rights And Faith-Based Clubs

CHAPTER 1

REACHING OUT: THE LIFELINE

Are You Concerned About Kids in Public School?

* Do you wonder how Christians fare in public school?
* What influence does the secular environment have on your kids?
* Do you want to witness to students and bring them hope?
* Are you afraid that your kids may become friends with the wrong kids?
* Does a secular environment concern you?
* Do you worry that they may lose their interest in God and church?
* What if they stop attending youth group?
* What if they get confused in a religiously pluralistic environment?
* What if they question the existence of God altogether?

These are good questions that should concern us all. Thankfully, there are very meaningful and easily do-able solutions.

You can't change the secular nature of our public schools, but you can change the micro environment of a student at the school. One of the easiest ways to do this is to form Christian clubs. Most people don't even know how easy and possible this is!

Clubs help students find other Christian friends and surround themselves with good people. This book is about how to set up and grow Christian clubs inside public schools so our kids can support and empower each other. It's like a Christian fortress to protect kids from negative influences as much as possible. From there you can branch out and do assemblies or mentoring, or have a lunch pizza fest to just love on students; or whatever God is putting on your heart.

This book will give you the keys to open school doors, so you can let God back in. Imagine, a Christian club which serves as a launchpad to touch the hearts of non-Christians who so desperately need the love of God. Just think about all the school shootings. What if those kids would have found the love of God. One of the schools where I did my student teaching observation had six suicides between the beginning of the school year and February 2018.[2] That's six suicides in six months. And a school where I was teaching just had a middle schooler accidentally shoot himself in the bathroom; he was obsessed with the Columbine shooter and wanted to beat that. That's just in our area. Only big school incidents make it to national news, but our schools are desperate nationwide. They need hope and love more than ever before. I have found we can provide it in a most unexpected way.

From Kindergarten to High School

When it comes to Christian clubs, most people think about high school first. Yes, our teenagers need that kind of support, but so do our elementary school kids. Why not make sure that they get a good start in school with the right friends. With young children, we might not notice the negative influences bad relationships can have on them. After all they are not yet interested in music, parties, or drugs. However, it's critical to be around people with good character from an early age.

Friends are a tremendous influence on kids in schools. Like a compass, friends can steer them in any direction. Kids get introduced to new things, starting early on with lying, cheating on tests, mean behavior, and later moving to provocative dressing, partying, alcohol and maybe even drugs. I know so many moms whose kids went astray because of bad friends; some of them looked good but were ultimately still a bad influence. My daughter, as I describe in a later chapter, hung out with the bad smart kids from speech club. They looked perfect and behaved

---

[2] Almasy, S. (2018). 6 teen suicides in 6 months in 1 Ohio school district.
Retrievable at:
https://www.cnn.com/2018/01/16/health/ohio-suicide-cluster/index.html

well. I invited them to my house to check them out and was impressed with their manners and command of speech. I thought I was so blessed. Then I realized they were systematically destroying her faith and even her relationship with me.

While offering sanctuary for Christians, shouldn't we also send out lifelines to non-Christians? Christian kids can be the light students need. Young people question life. They search for answers at any student age. Why not engage in their journey to adulthood and provide answers teachers may fear to tackle? We have the opportunity to offer another option to the secular nature of public schools. In this book, you will be equipped with step-by-step instructions on how to set up a club in a public school and learn how to find help from other people in the community and school. You will be well prepared to speak with the principal. By the time you're done reading this book, you will know your free speech rights. You will not be intimidated by someone mentioning the 'separation of church and state' nor by school administration concerned about 'violating the establishment clause,' or other things you may have heard erroneously about.

Reach Our Public School Kids with God's Love

You will feel empowered and emboldened to reach our kids in public schools with the powerful message of God. I will show you the far-reaching freedom Christians have in public schools. You will be astounded to find out how many federal and civic organizations support Christian students.

And you will be delighted to learn how we can freely share the love of God and pray with others. As long as the club is voluntary, and operates during non-instructional school hours, you are allowed to teach any Bible lesson and talk about God as if you were in church. Imagine the change in atmosphere if this was happening all across the country.

I want to empower you to be a support for our students. It's difficult to maintain faith in a secular environment without a Christian community. Whether you are a parent, grandparent, pastor, church leader or any concerned adult, you're called to live out the Great Commission. Why not be that salt and light our students so desperately need. Why travel afar to share the love of God when the opportunity is so huge in our backyard.

A High Schooler Puts It This Way:

"During hectic days, it can be difficult to find time to talk about topics that you care about deeply. Imagine being able to settle down in a classroom full of students who care about the same issues you do. You are given a full hour to debate and express your feelings about how to solve these problems and whom they affect."[3]

An open Christian environment even helps students solve personal problems and get support when needed. We need to bring hope into our schools. Our students are more confused than ever. Even our Christian students get confused when taught about gender identity issues. The Gay-Straight Alliance has set foot in most high schools and even middle schools in our nation. And most of the kids from those clubs are atheists often proactively dissuading Christians.

Many high schools already have Christian clubs. The content of this book will not only help establish a club but also help your resolve of maintaining a Christian club. You will understand your legal rights and how to navigate the gay-straight alliances and LGBT community. This book is not about judging any group but to fully describe the landscape of public middle and high schools we need to include the gay-straight clubs in our book.

The gay-straight alliance clubs are growing faster than our Christian clubs. Shouldn't we as Christians be there for our students? Maybe God has called you to do that. It's not rocket science, just a love for students to reach out and support them.

Elementary and Middle Schools

Very few elementary and middle schools have Christian clubs, despite the fact that they are extra beneficial at that age. One of the reasons fewer clubs exist in elementary schools is the fact that different laws apply. In high schools, most clubs are set up via the Equal Access Act (which will be further explained in a later chapter) However, for an elementary school club, the First Amendment's Free Speech and Free

---

[3] Martinez, J. (2017). Students connect in religious clubs.
Retrievable at:
https://thesagonline.com/25068/news/students-connect-in-religious-clubs

Exercise clauses apply. Parents, grandparents, pastors or youth leaders can run an elementary school club. So why not start one? You can structure it for as little as a six-week program, for one hour per week in Spring and Fall. In such little time, you can impact the life of a student forever. (More on this later.)

News and social media primarily report about the ACLU, the separation of church and state, and that prayer was taken out of school. But the fact is: We can have Christian clubs as a voluntary after-school activity in our public schools. Because of all the negative news surrounding God and public schools, most people don't even know this. I certainly didn't.

The Department of Education Endorses Christian Clubs

Most people also don't know that sixteen national agencies, including Federal agencies such as the Department of Education and the White House Office for Faith-based Partnership, fully endorse Christian clubs in schools, and even the ACLU has never once challenged them. You will be surprised to learn about the Supreme Court and key legal cases which brought us such freedom.

This book will show you what you can and cannot do in public schools. You will feel confident in your rights, whether you are a parent, student, teacher, counselor or principal. You will see more of those eye-opening statistics, and you will receive very specific guidelines about setting up a Christian club or maintaining a current one.

Join The Movement....

Thousands of such faith-based clubs already exist nationwide. Not only in high schools but even in elementary schools. Why not start one for your local school? This is especially vital if you live in a challenged area of town or feel called to work in one. You will hardly do anything else in life with better eternal results than engaging yourself with such open hearts and minds.

Do you like to work with elementary school kids? If yes, then start praying and asking God to show you in which school God wants you to be the light. You may be called to serve God's interest in high schools where you can help rescue souls and empower students. From an early age, our kids need to surround themselves with good friends. This holds true especially in public school settings where they're exposed and influenced by friends every day.

Your choice to act can make all the difference in a student's life, their friends lives, and even the families represented. Please join me to bring hope to our public schools!

CHAPTER 2

IS GOD STILL WELCOME IN PUBLIC SCHOOLS?

"Zack won't come for dinner. I think he's crying in his room?"

"Do you know what happened, Addie?"

"I think it's something with his girlfriend, cause he talked to her earlier on the phone. When I get that age I'll never have a boyfriend."

"Good idea, cause you know they have the cooties!"

"That's right, let's just eat without him. I'm hungry."

"Hey Zack, I've got a plate of food for you. Can I come in, please?"

"No, I'm not hungry. I want to be alone."

"Please, Zack. It helps to talk."

"Not right now, mom."

"Come on down honey. Give him space," his dad called up knowing his wife's face was pressed against Zack's door in agony. "Maybe it's even best if she breaks up with him. You know she's not the best influence on Zack, and she's not even a believer."

Wiping Claire's tears from her face, he knew he had to come up with a plan, "If Zack could just find other Christians in school."

"What about me?" Addie piped in, "Elementary school is not so easy either. Some of my friends are mean, and they don't even know that God loves them. I wish I could tell them about God, but I don't know how."

"Maybe we should start a Christian club in both elementary and high school," Mom said.

"I'd love to have a club like that in my school," Addie brimmed with hope.

"Is that even allowed? Didn't they take prayer out of school years ago and doesn't that mean you can't talk about God at all?" said dad.

Here's what the Clark family learned:

Can Students Talk About God In Public School or Meet In Christian Clubs?

Yes, thanks to the First Amendment of the Constitution of the United States.

Students do not, the Court tells us in Tinker vs. Des Moines[4] shed their constitutional rights when they enter the schoolhouse door."[5]

> . . In the absence of a specific showing of constitutionally valid reasons to regulate their speech, students are entitled to freedom of expression of their "views." Justice Fortas, speaking for the majority.

---

[4] Tinker v. Des Moines Indep. Community Sch. Dist., 393 U.S. 503, 506 (1969).
"John and Mary Beth Tinker of Des Moines, Iowa, wore black armbands to their public school as a symbol of protest against American involvement in the Vietnam War. When school authorities asked that the Tinkers remove their armbands, they refused and were subsequently suspended. The Supreme Court decided that the Tinkers had the right to wear the armbands, with Justice Abe Fortas stating that no one expects students to "shed their constitutional rights to freedom of speech or expression at the schoolhouse gate."
Retrievable at:
http://landmarkcases.org/en/Page/245/Summary_of_the_Decision
[5] Ibid. Justice Fortas, speaking for the majority.

The First Amendment's Free Speech and Free Exercise Clauses provide full protection of student religious speech in public schools. This includes all public schools from K-12.

Students can talk about their faith just like they can talk about any other subject in class. Faith can be expressed in assignments or classroom discussions as long as it does not interfere with classroom teaching or is disruptive. Students can mention a biblical principal even referring to the Bible when appropriate in a classroom discussion.

More than that, students are at liberty to enjoy their constitutional rights to freely exercise their faith by having Christian clubs at school.

Why then are so many people confused about Christian rights in Schools?

It's because teachers and students have different rights. Sadly, both of them often get lumped together resulting in contradictory information. Teachers and the whole school staff have much more limited rights to talk about God. Therefore students often get confused and think that their rights are limited as well. However, that is not the case! Why? Because students can fully exercise their Free Speech rights as outlined in the First Amendment.

The First Amendment not only contains the Free Speech Clause, it also contains the Establishment Clause. Teachers, unlike students, have to uphold the Establishment Clause, which prohibits the government from trying to establish a religion. School administrators, teachers, and school staff are more restricted as they act in an official government position and therefore are not permitted to endorse religion. The establishment clause prohibits the government, and by extension school personnel, from officially establishing one religion, denomination, or even atheism over another.

Students are not considered to be representatives of the government and can therefore never violate the establishment clause. It simply does not pertain to students. That's why students are fully permitted to freely focus on expressing their faith. (This also includes any parent or adult who is not a school employee but teaches a Christian club even in elementary school.)

Students are only limited in one area: they cannot disrupt the classroom. For example students can bring up faith as it pertains to a discussion in class, but they cannot start outright preaching during class. But outside of class, even that is not a problem as students can talk about their faith just like any other subject. That's why it makes sense for students to get together in Christian clubs.

So far it was easy, but now it gets a little tricky:

Even though the Free Speech Clause is sufficient to start a Christian club in all K-12 schools we have another piece of legislation effecting the boundaries. It applies only to secondary schools.

Equal Access Act

The Equal Access Act was passed by Congress in 1984 in the wake of discrimination against Christians in the two decades after prayer was taken out of school. Congress wanted to make it crystal clear that Christian clubs have the same rights as any other clubs. It grants equal access to Christian student groups to meet on campus just like any other nonreligious group. Students can meet during non-curriculum, non-instruction time, as long as it doesn't interfere with instruction. The club must be voluntary, student-led, and student-initiated. Non-students, such as youth leaders, may not set up, direct, control, conduct, or regularly attend the group. And students cannot invite the same speaker more than once every fourth meeting.

The fact that the club has to be student-led is what makes a club using the Equal Access Act difficult to implement. Some high school students who want to start a Christian club may be overwhelmed by the responsibility of having to lead it all by themselves. Furthermore, they may want some help from a more experienced adult. That's when high school students have and option to ask themselves the question:

Should I Use The First Amendment Rights or the Equal Access Act?

High school Christian clubs typically use the Equal Access Act to set up a Christian club because principals are more familiar with Equal Access clubs. In fact, most principals do not even know that it could be set up via the First Amendment Free Speech Rights.

As mentioned, the Equal Access Act option works well if students are comfortable enough to lead the club, since the Equal Access Act requires the club to be student led.

The Equal Access Act also works better if the principal is not supportive of Christianity. A principal can hardly say no to an Equal Access club. The First Amendment club has just as much legal standing, but you'd have to explain it to the principal who is primarily familiar with the Equal Access Act.

But what if students want more help from adults than is allowed under the Equal Access Act?

High school students who want to have more adult leadership can instead set up the club using the First Amendment Free Speech Rights just like the clubs are set up in elementary schools. The great benefit is that this will allow students to have adult leaders to help set up and run the club. Those adult leaders also are allowed to teach without limitations. But because secondary school administration might not be aware of such a club which is set up as a community club, you need to provide further information to the principal. All of this will be covered in a later chapter.

Elementary Schools Use First Amendment Rights

If you want to set up a club in an elementary school, you don't have to rack your brain about which way to set it up. You only have one option: Christian Clubs set up in elementary schools always use the First Amendment's Free Speech Rights and are set up as community clubs. Clearly, an elementary school club cannot be student led and therefore was never included in the Equal Access Act.

Typically parents, grandparents, youth leaders or other community leaders teach the club. Parental permission slips are attached to club flyers for parents to sign up their student. However, club participation still needs to be voluntary and during non-instructional time.

CHAPTER 3

WHAT ABOUT THE ACLU?

Or Americans United?

Or the Freedom from Religion Foundation?

Jenna Clarke and Robyn Krause talked about the worldly influence on their kids in school. They worried not only about their high schoolers but also wondered if they could help their elementary schoolers from slowly losing faith. After kicking the thoughts back and forth, the two realized it would be great to find other kids in school whose parents were open to a Christian club. This way their kids would find good friends, and they could even learn to share their faith with others. Still, the nagging questions arose: "Is it legal? Would the ACLU prevent it?", and "What if the principal is afraid of the ACLU or one of the other atheist groups it backs?" came up.

Words like 'school' and 'faith' conjure up images of the ACLU or one of its branches. News reports remind us how the ACLU challenges school prayer and school religious symbols. Schools often cave to the ACLU. "We would rather spend our money on teachers than on lawyers" is a frequent justification.

We see the ACLU backing the Freedom From Religion Foundation against our Christian traditions in schools. The ACLU also supports Americans United in many anti-Christian efforts. But, there is no need to fear the ACLU when it comes to Christian clubs. In fact, the ACLU officially acknowledges and supports Christian clubs in public schools.

Because students won numerous lawsuits against schools who denied Christian clubs, an increasing number of principals are focusing on protecting their students' rights to free speech. School administration is not alone in becoming more cognizant of student rights; even the ACLU schooled a school in the spring of 2014:

The American Civil Liberties Union (ACLU) of Tennessee stood up for the Christian rights of a student who was forced by teachers to stop reading the Bible during an After-School program.

In that situation, school personnel told an elementary school student that he was not allowed to read the Bible. When he refused to cave in to their demand, the teacher took the Bible away from him stating that the school could lose their funds if they allowed him to read the Bible.

Instead of turning to one of many excellent Christian legal organizations, the student's parents turned to the ACLU for help. Why? They must have been convinced of the student's constitutional right to exercise his faith. And they must have known that the ACLU had to back up their son's right to free exercise of his faith.

That is exactly what happened. The ACLU defended the student against the school.

In a letter sent to the school in April 2014, the ACLU requested that it's the school's "obligation under the law to safeguard their students' religious liberties - without imposing religion on them."[6]

To come into compliance with the law, the school responded by training its employees on religious freedom rights.

Students Have Constitutional Rights

"The First Amendment exists to protect religious freedom," said Thomas H. Castelli, ACLU-TN legal director. "While this means that schools may not impose or promote religion, it also means that students can

---

[6] Castelli, T. H. (2014). ACLU-TN protects student's right to read Bible in school. Retrievable at:
https://www.aclu.org/news/aclu-tn-protects-students-right-read-bible-school?

engage in religious activities that they initiate, provided they do not cause a disruption or interfere with the education of other students."[7] Those rights apply to non-instructional time such as lunch, recess and before/after-school time.

Hedy Weinberg, executive director of the ACLU's Tennessee branch, explained that "the goal of their letter was to clarify how constitutionally-guaranteed religious freedoms work. ACLU-TN has a long-standing commitment to uphold and defend Tennesseans' ability to practice religion, or not, as they choose."[8]

The ACLU Supported an Anti-Abortion Club

In May 2017, Parkland High School in Allentown, Pennsylvania, would not allow two students to start an anti-abortion club. Because the mother of one of the students had an abortion against her will when she was young, the students wanted to support other students who are in the same situation, but the school said, "the club was too controversial and too political."[9]

So they looked for legal help. Jocelyn Floyd, an attorney for the Thomas More Society, said in the Morning Call: "The law is clear and the lawyers know it. The school administrators are the ones who don't always understand what the obligations are under the law."[10]

The legal director of the ACLU of Pennsylvania, Vic Walczek, also thinks

---

[7] Castelli, T. H. (2014). ACLU Tennessee.

[8] Weber, K. (2014). Boy Forced to Stop Reading Bible During Tenn. After-School Program; ACLU Defends Student.
Retrievable at:
https://www.christianpost.com/news/boy-forced-to-stop-reading-bible-duringtenn-after-school-program-aclu-defends-student-117229/

[9] Allen, Michael (2017). High School Won't Allow Students' Anti-Abortion Club.
Retrievable at:
https://www.opposingviews.com/i/society/high-school-wont-allow-students-anti-abortion-club

[10] Wojcik, S. (2017). National law firm says Parkland violating law in rejecting pro-life student club.
Retrievable at:
http://www.mcall.com/news/local/parkland/mc-parkland-prolife-club-censored-20170517-story.html

that Parkland High School violated the Equal Access Act. Schools often use words such as: controversial, political, or illegal, to intimidate students simply because the administration doesn't want to deal with parents who might object to a Christian club.

But to be fair, it needs to be stated that most principals decide to uphold the First Amendment Rights of their students no matter who complains.

Nationally, the ACLU never directly challenged a Christian club in schools. All they ever filed was an amicus brief in the landmark case: Good News Club vs. Milford Central School.[11] However, the Supreme Court decided in favor of the Christian club.

The ACLU instead challenges Christian symbols in schools, such as the posting of the ten commandments or nativity scenes. The organization also likes to challenge Christian seals or Christian remarks in official school documents. And we all know the ACLU challenges mandatory school prayer.

Still, the ACLU fully recognizes and accepts Christian clubs in schools and respects students' constitutional rights. It's of paramount importance that we utilize this right to support our students.

---

[11] Good News Club et al. v Milford Central School, 533 U.S. 98 (2001)
Retrievable at:
http://caselaw.findlaw.com/us-supreme-court/533/98.html

CHAPTER 4

WHAT ABOUT SEPARATION OF CHURCH AND STATE?

Brittany looked on as her daughter boarded the school bus on the first day of school. She gave her a smile and a wave before heading back to the house, but Brittany's mind was full of worrisome thoughts. "What if she starts talking about God like she does at home? Will she get in trouble or even wind up in the principal's office? Or worse, what if she loses her faith?" Brittany was concerned. She didn't know who she could talk to about this situation. She didn't know any other Christian kids starting school that year, and she certainly couldn't ask the school office.

Brittany then remembered her son who had begun his first day of high school earlier that morning. She hoped he would stay away from negative influences and especially from drugs and alcohol. Suddenly alarmed she thinks, "What if he becomes a part of the gay-straight alliance?" Not that she thought they were inherently bad people, but she heard of that community having little tolerance towards Christians. Mostly, Brittany was wondering whether her son would stand firm in his faith, or if the separation of church and state would prevent him from talking about his faith.

Separation of church and state means that the government cannot exercise its authority in establishing a national religion.

Schools constitute a local extension of the government which cannot make religion mandatory for all students. That clause of the First Amendment is called the "Establishment Clause."

'Separation of church and state' is a well-known phrase. However, it is not found in the Constitution of the United States.

This term has been misinterpreted over the years and has evolved to the current interpretation demonstrated in the short story above. Our Founding Fathers never meant to separate state and church, but instead just wanted to make sure that the government does not interfere with religion. The original intent was that the government does not officially establish one particular religion or denomination over another or even establish non-religion over religion.

Here is the First Amendment Establishment Clause[12]

"Congress shall make no law respecting an establishment of religion, or prohibiting the free exercise thereof..."

Where, then, did the term "Separation of Church" originate?

It stems from Thomas Jefferson's use of the phrase "wall of separation between Church and State"[13] as he tries to explain the First Amendment religion clauses to the Danbury Baptist Association in a letter:

---

[12] Establishment Clause,
Retrievable at:
https://www.law.cornell.edu/wex/establishment_clause
[13] "The fact is there is nothing wrong with Jefferson referring to the Establishment Clause as a wall between church and state in his famous Danbury Baptists letter. Jefferson was simply describing in a colorful way disestablishment, which in simple words means religion can no longer be an auxiliary of government control.

The words "Congress shall make no law respecting an establishment of religion, or prohibiting the free exercise thereof," means in simple words that no power was invested in Congress to established a national church and to compel by law worship of its tenets, which in return disallows the "free exercise" of religion. This is the "wall" the First Amendment erects to which Jefferson referred.
Retrievable at:
http://www.federalistblog.us/2010/11/

"I contemplate with sovereign reverence that act of the whole American people which declared that their legislature should 'make no law respecting an establishment of religion, or prohibiting the free exercise thereof,' thus building a wall of separation between church and State."[14]

The first time the Supreme Court cited the phrase, "Wall of separation between church and state" was in 1947 in the case Everson versus Board of Education of Ewing.[15] Since this term did not exist in the Congressional records, they used it from the private letter of Jefferson to the Danbury Baptist Association quoted above.

Subsequently, the Supreme Court ruled that a wall of separation between church and state exists based on that personal letter rather than the Constitution. As a result, the Supreme Court created an erroneous precedent, ruling that law could be created from a personal letter instead of the Constitution.

Even if a letter was considered a law in the United States, the Supreme Court misinterpreted what Jefferson wrote. Jefferson's words were used as a legal precedent despite being used out of context. This redefinition of Jefferson's original meaning has provided the basis for the Supreme Court's definition of separation of church and state.

However, not one of the ninety Founding Fathers stated, argued for or against, or even referred to such a phrase when they debated for months about the specific words to use when writing the First Amendment. Congressional Records from June 7 to September 25, 1789, reveal that none of these men, including Thomas Jefferson, ever used the phrase, "separation of church and state." Two days after Jefferson wrote his "wall of separation" metaphor he attended church services held in the House of Representatives where the Speaker's podium served as the pulpit.

This was no isolated event either as he continuously attended church services held on government property during his two terms as President. President Madison also attended church services in the House on Sundays. Even the Treasury building was used as a church on Sundays

---

[14] Writings of Thomas Jefferson, 113 (H. Washington ed. 1861)
[15] Everson v. Board Of Education Of Ewing TP.330 U.S. 1, 15-16

where John Quincy Adams was known to attend.[16]

**The intent of our founding fathers was to
protect religion from the government not to exclude and separate
religion from government.**

But the Everson v Board of Education of Ewing case changed all that by introducing the term "separation of church and state" for the first time in history. While it does not appear that making religion an outlaw in public schools was the intent of the founders, nor was it the practice in America before 1947, the Everson case set the stage for other challenges to religious practices in public schools.

Daily prayer and Bible reading were challenged and dismissed from public schools in the early 1960s. Other forms of the official religious expression became legally unwelcome in public schools with the elimination of graduation prayers in 1992 and prayers before football games in 2000.

So the term 'separation of church and state' can be considered a misnomer because the founding fathers never wanted to entirely separate their Christian belief from government. They just didn't want the government to choose one denomination over another and make that the state church. They welcomed the Christian faith at large even within government walls. However, this term has been interpreted by our courts in a stricter way for some decades now.

**Our forefathers stated that violating the Establishment Clause means
that not one denomination should be established over another
denomination.**

But today the courts state that violating the Establishment Clause takes place when a government authorized person such as a teacher endorses faith or tries to establish religion on behalf of the government.

Shall We let The Separation of Church and State Issue

---

[16] Madison, P. A. (2010). The Federalist Papers 14th Amdt House Report (1871)

Separate Us?

The following section will show you the bigger picture and how you can make an impact despite the Separation of Church and State. You have so many free speech rights and full endorsements of all major government agencies as you will see in the next chapter. All of us have great opportunity to share pure faith which draws people in willingly and undergirds our Christian beliefs.

Religious Freedom for All

James Madison words were adopted into the Virginia Constitution Bill of Rights[17] and stated:[18]

> "That religion or the duty which we owe to our Creator, and the manner of discharging it, can be directed only by reason and conviction, not by force or violence; and, therefore, all men are equally entitled to the free exercise of religion, according to the dictates of conscience."

Evidently, those Founders believed in free will. That's why they wanted to make sure government would refrain from making religion mandatory. Rather, Christian faith should arise out of personal conviction.

The early Founders came out of Europe which was influenced by state churches. These government endorsed state churches levied mandatory church taxes on people. That's precisely what our Forefathers wanted to prevent in the new colonies. They were also skeptical of government's fingers making faith decisions which they believed should be reserved for clergy.

The state churches in Europe, to this day, work to some degree with the government. The Supreme Court in Germany, for instance, still decides if Catholic or Lutheran believers get to take sacraments if they choose

---

[17] Bill of Rights.
Retrievable at:
http://law.justia.com/constitution/virginia/constitution.html
[18] James Madison, A Memorial and Remonstrance Against Religious Assessments, addressed to the Virginia General Assembly, June 20, 1785

not to pay the church tax.[19] (And, by the way, the answer is "no.")

Another problem with state churches is that the government can influence the upper management of Christian hospitals, schools, charities and even churches. State churches are so entangled with politics that their very faith and doctrines are affected by political motives.

Such government-influenced and ecumenical movements can result in inadvertently supporting anti-Christian trends. Multiple agendas might interfere with making decisions based on faith only. Jesus had nothing good to say about the church-state connection of the Pharisees. Attending church for social reasons, position or prestige (which easily happens in a state church) can result in a watered down version of the gospel. God likes us all in or out, not half hearted.

But since you are like lukewarm water, neither hot nor cold, I will spit you out of my mouth! Rev. 3:16 NLT

Do we want to create lukewarm Christians who go through the motions of school prayer without truly seeking God? If religion is not mandated, people see a more loving and pure version of the faith. Should our glorious faith be reduced to an obligatory prayer people might resent? Would that be a religious performance with little substance? God detests false idols. Does God also detest false worship?[20]

In 1 Corinthians 13, Jesus tells us to be loving and kind. While we have our rights to exercise our Free Speech in schools, we need to be aware of being considerate towards others and their beliefs.

Instead, let's turn our eyes and hearts toward our full rights to exercise our faith through voluntary Christian clubs and inviting those nonbelievers who are truly interested?

Focus on the Free Speech and Exercise Clause

---

[19] Kaemper, O. (2012). Keine Sakramente nach Kirchenaustritt.
Retrievable at:
http://www.dw.com/de/keine-sakramente-nach-kirchenaustritt/a-16263114
[20] Ruth, J. (2016). One Nation under God . Lexington, KY., p. 62

The Supreme Court's interpretation of the separation of church and state focuses as much on guaranteeing the free exercise of faith as it does on making sure it's not government endorsed.

"Congress shall make no law prohibiting the free exercise thereof..."

The focus of this book is not to challenge interpretations of separation of Church and State, but to fully utilize the right to free speech and free exercise of faith. Students have the right and opportunity to freely meet and discuss faith on school grounds. Our courts and schools have faithfully upheld this right. It makes more sense to me to work on establishing and growing Christian clubs instead of debating about whether the Supreme Court was right in how they interpreted Jefferson statement.

Respecting the Supreme Court Decision

Even though we might not agree with the Supreme Court decision, we need to consider Jesus' teaching on the temple tax in Matt. 17: 24:

> "After Jesus and his disciples arrived in Capernaum, the collectors of the two-drachma temple tax came to Peter and asked, "Doesn't your teacher pay the temple tax?"

> "Yes, he does," he replied.

> When Peter came into the house, Jesus was the first to speak "What do you think Simon, he asked, from whom do the kings of the earth collect duty and taxes—from their children or others?"

> "From others," Peter answered.

> "Then the children are exempt," Jesus said to him.

> "But so that we may not cause offense, go to the lake and throw out your line. Take the first fish you catch; open its mouth, and you will find a four-drachma coin. Take it and give it to them for my tax and yours."

Jesus did not agree with paying the tax, but he still instructed Peter to pay the tax to avoid people being offended. In the same vein, we need to respect the Supreme Court decision about separation of church and state and how they applied it to the Establishment Clause.

But keep in mind that separation of church and state only affects Christian teachers, staff, and administration - not our students. Our students can never violate the establishment clause because they are not held to those standards. Instead, let's focus on the task at hand of helping our students with the rights we are given. There is great legal protection in the Free Speech and Free Exercise clauses. They create opportunities that are vastly underemployed.

Setting up and growing Christian clubs in schools does not violate the establishment clause nor does it violate the separation of church and state. Christian clubs are regulated and fully endorsed by the Free Speech and Free Exercise Clauses. Separation of church and state only applies to school staff, not students.

Recent Ruling on the Separation of Church and State:

At a time when Americans are deeply divided over the meaning of "separation of church and state," a ruling from the 2nd U.S. Circuit Court of Appeals in 2014 provides a much-needed case study in how the First Amendment's establishment clause is supposed to work.

In a unanimous decision, the three-judge panel dismissed a challenge by atheists to the display of a cross-shaped beam at the National Sept. 11 Memorial and Museum at Ground Zero in New York City.

As the court explained, "the Establishment Clause is not properly construed to command that government accounts of history be devoid of religious references." The First Amendment, in other words, separates church from state – but not religion from public life.[21]

---

[21] Haynes, C. (2014). "Cross at Ground Zero": History Lesson or State Religion? Retrievable at:
http://www.firstamendmentcenter.org/cross-at-ground-zero-history-lesson-or-state-religion

CHAPTER 5

WHICH ORGANIZATIONS SUPPORT CHRISTIAN RIGHTS?

As the mothers started to research, they were astounded by how many organizations, including government authorities, endorse Christian clubs in our public schools. Here is a list of them:

Supreme Court

Supreme Court Verdict States: Religious Clubs Can Meet At Public Schools

> "The Supreme Court ruled in favor of a voluntary Christian club which meets during non-instructional time and inside the school facilities. The majority found that excluding the club was unconstitutional discrimination based on the club's views. Letting the meeting take place would not be an unconstitutional government endorsement of religion, the court ruled."[22]

NEA

The National Education Association Is Pulling In Faith-Based Organizations to Improve Student Learning In Their Priority Schools Campaign

---

[22] United States Supreme Court, Good News Club et al. v. Milford Central School[1], (2001)
Retrievable at:
http://caselaw.findlaw.com/us-supreme-court/533/98.html

"Building collaborations with community partners: Pulling in strategic partners and developing community by-in with colleges, social service agencies, community groups, faith-based organizations, local leaders, public officials, and businesses - to improve student learning and other outcomes."

Department of Education

Promotes Student Achievement by Connecting Schools with Faith-Based Organizations[24]

"The mission of the Center for Faith-based and Neighborhood Partnerships at the U.S. Department of Education is to promote student achievement by connecting schools and community-based organizations, both secular and faith-based."

The White House Office of Faith-Based Partnerships[25]

States That Faith And Community Groups Are Critical Partners In Expanding Community Involvement.[26]

"Education is a critical pathway to success for individuals and families. Partnerships between schools and faith-based and community organizations can help to achieve this goal of educational success for

---

[23] Anne T. Henderson, Senior Consultant to the Annenberg Institute for School Reform, and co-author of A New Wave of Evidence: The Impact of School, Family, and Community Connections on Student Achievement and Beyond the Bake Sale: The Essential Guide to Family-School-Community Partnerships 2.0. National Education Association (NEA) 2011
Retrievable at:
http://www.nea.org/assets/docs/Family-School-Community-Partnerships-2.0.pdf
[24] Faith-based and Neighborhood Partnerships .
Retrievable at:
http://sites.ed.gov/fbnp/
[25] (2018). Faith-based and Neighborhood Partnerships.
Retrievable at:
http://sites.ed.gov/fbnp/
[26] President Obama, (2010). PARTNERSHIPS for the COMMON GOOD.
Retrievable at:
https://obamawhitehouse.archives.gov/sites/default/files/faithbasedtoolkit.pdf

all students. That is why the Center for Faith-Based and Neighborhood Partnerships at the Department of Education works to promote student achievement and build a culture of educational excellence within communities across the country."

"The White House Office of Faith-based and Neighborhood Partnerships works to build bridges between the federal government and nonprofit organizations, both secular and faith-based, to better serve Americans in need. The Office advances this work through Centers in various Federal agencies."

The NEA Foundation

States That Successful School Districts Have Relied On Faith-Based Institutions[27]

"Successful union and district collaborations have included creation of partnerships with community-based organizations, faith-based institutions, health and mental health agencies, and city- or community-based agencies focused on developing comprehensive solutions for the complex challenges of educating all students."

NEA Today

Encourages Schools To Develop Meaningful Partnerships With Faith Organizations[28]

"Local Partnerships to Transform Priority Schools. Partnerships between priority schools and their communities help students succeed—in school and in life."

"While some local associations and school districts are in the beginning phases of developing meaningful partnerships with local businesses, civic, faith and social organizations, and community coalitions, several priority schools are already seeing the benefits these

---

[27] The NEA Foundation Report (2012, April). Expanding Learning Opportunities to Close The Achievement Gaps: Lessons from Union-District Collaborations. Retrievable at:
http://www.neafoundation.org/content/assets/2012/04/elo-final-2.pdf
[28] Buffenbarger, A. (2011). Faith-based and Neighborhood Partnerships. Retrievable at:
http://www.nea.org/tools/48684.htm

partnerships can have for their students."

ACLU

States That: "Student-Organized Bible Clubs[29] Are Ok As Long As Three Conditions Are Met:

- ◆ the activity must take place during non-school hours
- ◆ school officials can't be involved in organizing or running the club
- ◆ the school must make its facilities available to all student groups on an equal basis.

Pastors, Churches, Educators And Volunteers Support Christian Involvement In Schools

According To A Barna[30] Research Report From 2014:

95% of pastors believe that Christians should get involved in helping public schools.

80% of church-going Christians across all denominations feel the same way.

50% of public school teachers attend church at least monthly

65% of public school volunteers are Christians

50% of churches offer support for educators who attend their church

25% of churches offer mentoring or after-school programs

Reasons Why People Don't Volunteer In Public Schools

[29] (2018)YOUR RIGHT TO RELIGIOUS FREEDOM.
Retrievable at:
https://www.aclu.org/other/your-right-religious-freedom
[30] (2014) Public Schools: Christians are part of the solution.
Retrievable at:
https://www.barna.com/research/public-schools-christians-are-part-of-the-solution/

According To Barna:

44% say they don't have children in the school

18% say public schools don't want Christians to help

17% don't know how to help

16% say the public school needs more prayer and religious values, not academic support

6% public school is contrary to their belief

7% doubt they can make a long-term difference[31]

---

[31] percentages don't necessarily add up because people could choose more than one category.

CHAPTER 6

KEY SUPREME COURT CASE STORY

Connecting With Community

Darleen Fournier, along with her husband Rev. Stephen Fournier, wanted to be active in their community and be a blessing to people. They had just moved to Milford to pastor a church and hoped to connect with others in town. Darleen found another woman with whom she shared the same desire and they established a Christian club at their Community Bible Church for elementary school students. After all, the Fourniers' two daughters attended the local elementary school. The club provided character education through faith-based stories, games, scripture, and songs. Parental permission was required before joining the club. It was open to all faiths or even non-faiths and stayed clear from denominational doctrines.

The Club was right after school, and parents let their children go straight to the church via the school bus since the church was a regular bus stop for the Fourniers' daughters. Parents then picked up their children at the church when the club was over. Kids were having fun while learning morals and character from a Christian perspective. The club became popular.

The School Superintendent Stepped In

Soon, the interim superintendent of Milford Schools decided against letting the students out at the Fourniers' bus stop. No specific reason was given, but the kids were told that there was no longer room on the bus. However, the Boy Scouts were still allowed to use the bus to transport the students to their meetings.To alleviate the transportation problems, the Fourniers decided to bring the club right to the school premises. According to school policy a proper "building use form" was submitted which is used by all outside organizations wanting to use school buildings for community meetings. Stephen and Darleen Fournier were school district residents and therefore eligible to use the school's facilities upon approval of their proposed use. However, the building use request was not approved. The Fourniers communicated to the school that they were surprised the school allowed other clubs while denying theirs simply because of the Christian perspective. The school board stated that "the kinds of activities proposed to be engaged in by the Good News Club were not a discussion of secular subjects such as child rearing, development of character and development of morals from a religious perspective, but were, in fact, the equivalent of religious instruction itself." The Milford School Board unanimously denied the request stating that these activities are equivalent to religious worship which is prohibited in their Community Use Policy.

Communications Problems

Neither the superintendent nor the school board president agreed to a meeting to discuss the situation. That's when the Fourniers realized they needed help and found the Rutherford Institute. A letter was sent to the school to help remedy the problem. Not only did the school continue to block any amicable efforts, but the school board president was wondering about where the club would find financial support for a legal defense. This resulted in the Rutherford Institute drafting a legal plan to address the issue.

In January 1997, a legal suit was filed by the Fourniers and the Good News Club[32] in the United States District Court for the Northern District of New York against Milford Central School. The Fourniers alleged that the school violated the free speech rights of the First Amendment, as well as the Religious Freedom Restoration Act. The suit went all the way up to the Supreme Court and was decided in 2001 in favor of the Christian club.

The Supreme Court ruled that the Christian club's religious speech rights

---

[32] Good News Club et al. v Milford Central School, 533 U.S. 98 (2001)
Retrievable at:
http://caselaw.findlaw.com/us-supreme-court/533/98.html

need to be upheld by the school. The court used the First Amendment's Free Speech right; the Religious Freedom Restoration Act was not needed to make the case.

The Rocky Road to the Supreme Court

The Fourniers and the Good News Club lost the first case in the Northern District of New York and turned around and filed an appeal with the 2nd Circuit Court of Appeals. But they also lost that case as the Second Circuit affirmed the District Court's holding that the school's restriction was not unreasonable. The woman who helped teach at the Club with Darleen was disappointed, and as a result, discontinued, not wanting to be involved in more legal matters.

Still, the Fourniers and the Good News Club decided not to give up because in a precedent case the 8th Circuit Court held that it is unconstitutional for schools to turn down clubs when others are allowed. Since both the 2nd and the 8th Circuit Courts dealt with similar subjects but rendered different opinions the issue needed to be decided by a higher court. That road led to the Supreme Court.

As a result of this split among the federal appeals courts on the question whether speech can be excluded from a limited public forum due to its religious content, the Supreme Court decided to accept and review the case.

The Supreme Court agreed to hear the case, and it was decided on June 11, 2001. The verdict was that Christian clubs are allowed in public schools and receive the same free speech rights as any other club. This case has since served as precedent. The Supreme Court held, "By denying the Club access to the school's limited public forum on the ground that the Club was religious in nature, Milford discriminated against the Club because of its religious viewpoint in violation of the Free Speech Clause."

The United States Supreme Court Ruled:

♦   Milford School violated the Free Speech Clause by restricting the Club
♦   The school board's decision and policy to deny the club were unconstitutional.

- Milford discriminated against the club because of the club's religious viewpoint, a violation of the Free Speech Clause.
- Permitting the club to meet in the school did not violate the Establishment Clauseand should, therefore, have been allowed by the school.

The Supreme Court decided that there is no difference between the viewpoint discrimination of this case and prior cases such as Lamb's Chapel v. Center Moriches Union Free School District[33] and Rosenberger[34] v University of Virginia.[35]

In Lamb's Chapel, the court held that a school violated the First Amendment's Free Speech Clause by denying a group the right to show a faith-based movie just because it had a Christian perspective. In Rosenberger, the court held that the denial of a university to fund a student publication because of its religious perspective violated the Free Speech Clause and constituted viewpoint discrimination. The Supreme Court applies the "strict scrutiny" standard when deciding on viewpoint discrimination. A denial of Christian clubs must be justified by a compelling governmental interest such as national security, preserving the lives of multiple individuals, and not violating explicit constitutional

---

[33] Lamb's Chapel v. Center Moriches Union Free School District, 508 U.S. 384 (1993) Retrievable at:
https://www.law.cornell.edu/supremecourt/text/508/384

[34] "A group of students formed a Contracted Independent Organization (CIO) at the University of Virginia, entitled Wide Awake Productions (WAP), which was organized for the purpose of publishing a magazine, which expressed Christian philosophical and religious viewpoints. When the Petitioners, Rosenberger and other members of WAP (Petitioners), submitted for funds from the Student Activities Fund (to which they were entitled, due to their CIO status) for printing costs, they were summarily turned down, because their publication expressed religious viewpoints, which might be construed as the views of the public university. The Petitioners filed suit, alleging that the Respondents, the Rector and Visitors of the University of Virginia's (Respondent), refusal to allot them a portion of the Student Activities Funds was an abridgment of their First Amendment Rights."
The Supreme Court ruled in favor of the Students.
Retrievable at:
https://www.casebriefs.com/blog/law/constitutional-law/constitutional-law-keyed-to-cohen/religion-and-the-constitution/rosenberger-v-rector-and-visitors-of-the-university-of-virginia-2/

[35] Rosenberger v. University of Virginia, 515 U.S. 819 (1995)
Retrievable at:
https://en.wikipedia.org/wiki/Rosenberger_v._University_of_Virginia

protections. The policy must also be the least restrictive means of achieving that interest.[36]

The Supreme Court held that Milford School Discriminated Against the Christian Club

The Supreme Court concluded that "Milford's exclusion is indistinguishable from the exclusions at issue in Lamb's Chapel and Rosenberger" and that the Court already decided in these prior cases that this violates the Free Speech Clause and applies to Milford the same way.

"'Milford has opened its limited public forum to activities that serve a variety of purposes, including events pertaining to the welfare of the community." Milford had asserted before the Second Circuit that it would have allowed a public group to use Aesop's fables to impart moral values to children. Milford also allowed the Boy Scouts to "influence a boy's character, development, and spiritual growth."[37]

Likewise, the Good News Club sought to teach moral values to children, albeit from an explicitly Christian viewpoint. The Court held that there is no difference between the Christian movies in Lamb's Chapel and the teachings of the Good News Club. According to the court majority, Milford, just like Lamb's Chapel and Rosenberger engaged in viewpoint discrimination. Milford violated the Free Speech Clause by engaging in viewpoint discrimination when adding to their school policy that the "school premises shall not be used by any individual or organization for religious purposes."

The Christian Club was Allowed Back in School

Therefore the Christian Club was allowed back into Milford school. Students have been blessed for many years now by the club's teaching,

---

[36] "Strict scrutiny is the most rigorous form of judicial review. The Supreme Court has identified the right to vote, the right to travel, and the right to privacy as fundamental rights worthy of protection by strict scrutiny."
Retrievable at:
http://legal-dictionary.thefreedictionary.com/Strict+Scrutiny
[37] Good News Club et al. v Milford Central School, 533 U.S. 98 (2001)
Retrievable at:
http://caselaw.findlaw.com/us-supreme-court/533/98.html

and Darleen is still teaching the club to this day. The Club has made a tremendous difference in students' lives as they learn about Christian morals and love. They also help guide those young lives to get a good start early in life.

The Court also held that no Establishment Clause violation exists since the club has equal access to the school facilities with other groups. If the school stays neutral toward religion, it is not trying to establish religion in schools nor entangling itself with the church. The Court held that approving the Good News Club would not favor religion over any other group since the limited public forum had already opened the door to other groups.

The Supreme Court disagreed with the school's argument that the young students would consider the presence of a religious club as an endorsement by the school. The Court held that if it were so, then education would be the answer, not censorship and that schools should teach about the difference between voluntary and mandatory activities.

"Allowing the Club to speak on school grounds would ensure, not threaten, neutrality toward religion."[38] The court also held that if students would consider a religious club as an endorsement by the school, they would equally consider the denial of a religious club as an endorsement and infer that the school is hostile towards religion.

---

[38] Ibid.

CHAPTER 7

HOW YOU CAN MAKE A DIFFERENCE

Who Will Rebuild The Wall?

Our adversity is an opportunity. As we view the tumbled walls of the moral structure in our society, we have a choice of throwing up our arms in despair or rolling up our sleeves to reach out and rebuild strong new walls founded on Christ the cornerstone.

Let's consider Nehemiah's example. He decided to rebuild the walls of Jerusalem which lay in ruin, but first, he had to be sensitive to the need and see the city from God's perspective. It's no wonder why he wept over the city when he heard of its decay. Nehemiah's heart for God and the city brought him to his knees, and later to action to restore God's vision for Jerusalem. His blueprints for rebuilding were God's heart and destiny for Jerusalem. God used Nehemiah to restore His holy city to holy use.

We must know and understand God's heart for students and our cities. He desires His godly character and destiny for both. We are called as the salt and the light to bring the solutions. We can bring God back into the public schools in our cities - and you can be the agent of change. Are you willing to help rebuild the wall? Sixteen federal agencies specifically call upon faith-based organizations to stand in the gap and bring solutions to our public schools and keep them safe. This is your hour to stand in the gap. Are you ready?

Make Your Life Count

All you need is a desire to reach out to all public school students. Consider just elementary school kids. They still want to be loved. This age group is spellbound hearing Bible stories. Elementary school children are old enough to behave in class and yet understand about God.

Every student should have the opportunity to hear about God's amazing love. The doors to public schools are open! This may be the greatest opportunity for fulfillment in your life while making eternal life impact on children!

It just takes
One person
One smile
One ear
One day to
Change the
Course of a
Student's life

Wisdom In Making Decisions

God promises to guide us in this venture! 1 John 5:14-15 states: "This is the confidence that we have in Him, that, if we ask anything according to His will, He hears us: and if we know that he hears us, whatsoever we ask, we know that we have the petitions that we desired of him."

We need to pray for divine favor. As we pray and listen to God, He will make a way, and He will provide the wisdom we need. If we ask Him what person of the administration to approach first, He will nudge us in the right direction, be it through an impression in our hearts, or through the conversation of a friend, or through reading the Bible.

"For the Lord grants wisdom! His every word is a treasure of knowledge and understanding. He grants good sense to the godly. He holds success in store for the upright; He is a shield to those whose walk is blameless." Proverbs 2:6-7

We can never lean on God too much or ask too many questions. He holds the ultimate wisdom, and He is so willing to share it with us. God is waiting for you to ask the questions that are on your heart—even specific questions like what person shall I approach and when. You cannot go wrong in discussing things with God in prayer and run things by him. He will give you peace with one decision over the other.

It is especially rewarding if you have another friend or mother to join you in your prayer and planning. "Two have good reward for their labor." (Ecc.4:9)

It's wise to go with His guidance. Since I have an MBA, I have made this mistake many times in my past. I always think I know what to do. But when things don't work out, I often realize that I should have asked God because He has called me and holds the ultimate wisdom.

In Job 12:13 it says: "But the true wisdom and power are God's. He alone knows what we should do; He understands."

Proverbs 2:9–10 states: "He shows how to distinguish right from wrong, how to find the right decision every time. For wisdom and truth will enter the very center of your being, filling your life with joy." The brother of Jesus says it this way: "If any of you lacks wisdom, they should ask God, who gives generously to all without finding fault, and it will be given to that person." James 1:5

I have often been astounded about King David always taking time to ask God. Many times, the enemy battalions were already approaching when David decided to stop and pray. To me, this seemed a simple decision— 'we need to defend ourselves.' But David was never presumptuous. No matter how urgent the situation or how easy this decision appeared, he stopped to pray, and God answered him every single time. Sure enough, sometimes he wasn't supposed to go and even defend his people. Other times God told him exactly to go this way and then that way. He gave him a whole strategic plan.

That's what God wants to do for you. He will give you wisdom if you ask Him. Here is how David looked at it: "I will bless the Lord who counsels me; He gives me wisdom in the night. He tells me what to do". Psalm 16:7

Don't Let Fear Talk You Out Of It

"Greater is He that is in you than he that is in the world." (1 John 4:4)

We need to embrace the winning attitude by knowing that God has already won the victory for us. His burden is light, and He will carry it for us. He is asking for a willing vessel, and He will do it through us.

Paul said: "Timothy, keep what has been entrusted to you" (1. Tim.6:20). Perhaps God is entrusting a certain school or specific students to you. Can you see your name instead of Timothy's in that verse? God most certainly has entrusted something to you. The question is what.

Leaders

You are reading this book for a reason. God led you to it and will enable you to stand in the gap for public school students. If God has called you, He will help you bring it about, but you still need the courage to get it started. God rewarded Joshua for seeing the possibilities, not the giants.

The Lord gave this command to Joshua son of Nun: "Be strong and courageous, for you will bring the Israelites into the land I promised them on oath, and I myself will be with you." (Deut. 31:23)

With the overwhelming bad news we hear daily, it's easy to feel like we could never make a difference. But God loves those odds! He is thrilled with those who heed the call and will give you the courage, confidence and strategy you need.

You were born for such a time as this. What is your calling?

"You are the light of the world. A city set on a hill cannot be hidden; nor does anyone light a lamp and put it under a basket, but on the lamp stand, and it gives light to all who are in the house. Let your light shine before men in such a way that they may see your good works, and glorify your Father who is in heaven." Matthew 5:14-16

PART TWO

Rights In Public Schools

CHAPTER 8

STUDENT RIGHTS K-12 FAQS

Can students pray in school?

Students can pray in school as long as it does not disrupt the class. Prayer before lunch or a test is certainly allowed. Students can also pray in groups during non-instructional time as long as it is not disruptive and is student initiated.

Can students express their religious beliefs in class or an assignment?

Students are welcome to express their religious beliefs in a class discussion or as part of an assignment when it pertains to the topic. Teachers and administrators cannot discriminate against religious expression as long as it falls within the guidelines of the project.

Can students express their religious beliefs in a school-wide talent show?

Yes. Talent shows offer students the ability to share about themselves. They can sing and dance to Christian music or recite Christian poems. Their talent falls into the Free Speech category and is therefore protected by the Constitution.

May students bring their Bible to school and read it in school?

Both carrying a Bible and reading it in school are constitutionally protected Free Speech rights routinely upheld by courts. Students' Free Speech rights would be violated if the students were not permitted to bring a Bible to school or to read it at appropriate times in school. *Schools are not religion-free zones.*

Can the school prohibit Bible clubs?

The First Amendment to the United States Constitution states: "Congress shall make no law.... Abridging the freedom of speech..... Or prohibiting the free exercise thereof."

Therefore public schools cannot suppress student speech because it's religious. Public schools are prohibited from discriminating against Free Speech including religious speech.

A school may not prohibit student expression during non-instructional time unless it (1) materially and substantially interferes with the operation of the school, or (2) infringes on the rights of other[39] students. A school may not prohibit student expression solely because others might find it offensive.[40] Christian Clubs can therefore not be prohibited.

Can a Christian club use promotional materials to spread the word about meetings or activities?

The right to freedom of speech has always included the right to communicate, promote and advertise. This right is supported by both the Equal Access Act and the First Amendment Free Speech Clause.
All Student clubs, including religious clubs, have the right to distribute materials, use bulletin boards, the school newspaper and even use the public address system to advertise their meetings and events. Schools may request a clarifying statement such as *"this is not a school-sponsored event."*

Can students gather anywhere on the school campus or do they have to be restricted to a certain location or room?

Students can spontaneously gather in groups at lunch or during any non-instructional time or free period. It's just like students in a group

---

[39] Tinker, 393 U.S. at 509
Retrievable at:
https://supreme.justia.com/cases/federal/us/393/503/case.html
[40] Morse v. Frederick, 127 S. Ct. 2618, 2629 (2007) (rejecting use of "offensiveness" standard for regulating student speech because "much political and religious speech might be perceived as offensive to some"); Nuxoll v. Indian Prairie Sch. Dist., 523 F. 3d 668, 672 (7th Cir. 2008)

taking about sports, social media or music. Students can talk about anything in small or large groups, whether organized or spontaneous, as long as it does not disrupt academics.

Regular gathering places for clubs are decided by the school administration. However, the club cannot be banned to the furthest room if more convenient rooms are available.

CHAPTER 9

STUDENT RIGHTS ELEMENTARY AND MIDDLE SCHOOL FAQS

Can elementary schools form Bible clubs?

Yes, even in elementary schools, students have the right to form clubs. These clubs also need to be voluntary and have to be offered during non-instructional time. They can meet inside or outside the school. In elementary schools, parents make the decision about joining the club. Students will bring home an invitation to the club with a sign-up portion of the flyer which is then returned to the school. This way, only students with parental permission can attend the club.[41]

Who can establish an elementary school faith-based club?

Typically parents, pastors, or youth leaders establish the clubs. At the elementary school level, the club does not have to be student led. Instead, the club communicates with the parents and obtains parental approval for the program that the club teacher proposes.

How are elementary school Christian clubs formed?

Elementary school Christian clubs are organized as community groups via the First Amendment's Free Speech Clause. (The Equal Access Act does not apply to elementary schools). The Club Teacher will request a community " facility use" form for using the school facility. But a meeting with the principal comes first. Club Organizers obtain approval

---

[41] Good News Club v. Milford Central School202 F.3d 502 (2d Cir. 2000), disapproved on other grounds, 533 U.S. 98 (2001).

from the principal for an after-school faith-based club according to Free Speech rights. The principal will approve the flyer so it can be distributed to all students. A parental sign up portion is part of the flyer which will be returned to school. This sign up signature also constitutes permission from the parent to faith-based teaching in the club. School sponsors are not needed because parents give permission for their child to attend the program. This will be explained in much greater detail later on in the Elementary and Middle School section of the book.

Some elementary school principals prefer to have a Christian program be part of their enrichment program or their after-school program. Schools send a program out to the parents listing all the classes students can take with the sign-up form attached. This works just as an individual form going out to the parents. In all cases, it's important to mention that this is a faith-based club. This will guarantee that only students whose parents want them in a Christian activity will attend. As the flyer explains, these clubs will freely talk about God.

Chapter 10

STUDENT RIGHTS IN HIGH SCHOOL

What laws apply to high schools?

Christian rights in high schools are not only protected by the Free Speech Clause of the First Amendment, but also by the Equal Access Act. This act was passed by Congress in 1984 to make sure that Christian clubs have the same rights as any other club in high school.[42]

If the school has other non-curricular clubs can we have a Christian club?

As long as even *one single other non-curricular club* in the school exists such as a chess club, a drama club or football team, the school has to allow a Christian club.

What is a non-curricular club?

If the club is not related to a specific class or subject area and the teacher does not require attendance (or give grades or assignments), the club is a non-curricular club.

---

[42]

In Mergens, Justice O'Connor, speaking for a four-Justice plurality, stated that "there is a crucial difference between government speech endorsing religion, which the Establishment Clause forbids, and private speech endorsing religion, which the Free Speech and Free Exercise Clauses protect." 496 U.S. at 259-60, 110 S. Ct. at 2372 (plurality opinion); see also id. 496 U.S. at 250, 110 S. Ct. at 2377 (Kennedy, J., concurring)
Retrievable at:
http://law.justia.com/cases/federal/appellate-courts/F3/28/1501/581520/

What is a "Limited Open Forum"?

When the school establishes its first non-curricular club, it automatically creates a "Limited Open Forum." If the school has created a limited open forum and receives Federal Assistance (which most schools do), then the Equal Access Act applies. The Equal Access Act guarantees that other clubs such as a Christian club have the same access to school facilities and enjoy the same benefits. This term only applies to the Equal Access Act in High Schools.

Which school rules have to be observed for a Christian club using the Equal Access Act?

The Christian Club has to:

◆ Be voluntary and meet during non-instructional time, such as lunch time, free periods or before or after school.
◆ Be student initiated and student led.
◆ Make sure that outside speakers cannot participate on a regular basis or more than once a month. However, speakers can be rotated as long the same speaker is not participating more than once a month.
◆ Be aware that school staff can only be present to maintain order, not to participate.
◆ Maintain order and discipline at all times to protect students, staff and property. Disorderly conduct is the only reason a club can be terminated.

Which school rules have to be observed for a Christian club using the First Amendment Free Speech Clause?

1. Be voluntary
2. Meet during non-instructional time

Can a Christian club meet in the classroom or other school facility?

Students can request the library, cafeteria, gym, classroom, etc. The school administration has to make every effort to accommodate the club within the requirements of other school activities. The Equal Access Act states that non-curriculum related clubs are allowed to meet on campus during non-instructional time such as before/after-school, free time, or lunch time.

Can the school limit the time or place students are allowed to meet in school?

A school can place limits on clubs as long as all clubs are treated equally. If the Christian club cannot use the library or cafeteria, then none of the other clubs can use them. Similarly, schools might have a policy which states that all clubs should be finished at a certain time after school.

Can a Christian club use school audio/visual equipment?

If the school allows other clubs to use supplies or equipment, then the school cannot discriminate against the Christian club according to the free-speech clause.

However, under the Equal Access Act, schools are not required to use public funds other than the basic cost of making space available. But again, if they make it available to other clubs, they need to grant you equal access.

Why do some school officials try to block a club?

They might be philosophically against a Christian club or be worried about offending atheists or the LGBT community. School officials may not be that familiar with the law themselves and merely need to be reminded that Christian clubs are legal.

What are some of the reasons school officials give for not allowing clubs?

Even though there are thousands of Bible clubs in U.S. high schools and the law is very clear about the legality of the clubs, some school officials are reluctant to allow them. They might state that certain parents will complain, or that all clubs have to be curriculum related, or that there is not a suitable space or supervision for the club. However, these are illegal obstacles.

What if the principal won't allow the club because it might endorse religion?

The Supreme Court ruled that equal access does not constitute the endorsement of religion. Allowing equal access to Christian clubs merely shows neutrality towards religion, not an endorsement of it.

What if a principal flat out refuses the Christian club?

Only two options exist for a principal to shut down a Christian club. Either the principal would have to close down all existing non-curricular clubs such as the chess club, drama club, and even the football team. Otherwise, the school would have to forgo federal funding.

If those clubs are not shut down nor the federal funds sent back, then the principal has no right to discriminate against the Christian club.

You may then need to politely bring documentation of legal cases which fully interpret the Equal Access Act and the First Amendments Free Speech Clause. Many principals are not up on the law and just need to find out the facts. The information provided in this book should be sufficient.

If they still refuse after such a meeting, then you can contact Christian legal organizations such as *Liberty Counsel*,[43] *Alliance Defending Freedom*,[44] *or the Christian Law Association*[45] to send a letter to the school on your behalf. Those organizations can send a demand letter to the school demanding your Christian rights to be honored.

However, it's best to be prepared and provide documents at the first meeting with the principal before a decision is made against a club.

Even if a Christian club is permitted, some school administrators may try to limit the club's rights.

Some schools may prohibit clubs from participating in club fairs or open houses or deny access to distribute materials or the PA system. They may prevent the club's picture from being placed in the yearbook or they may prevent the club's funds from being included in school accounts for clubs.

---

[43] http://libertycounsel.com
[44] http://adflegal.org
[45] http://www.christianlaw.org/cla/

All of these endeavors try to limit faith-based clubs and are illegal for any club whether it's a Free Speech Club or an Equal Access Club.

Why does the club have to be student led?

At the high school level, students can use two legal paths for a Christian club. The first path is via the First Amendment Free Speech Clause. And the second one is via the Equal Access Act.

If the Equal Access Act is invoked, then the students need to adhere to its guidelines. The Equal Access Act requires that adults are only present in a non-participatory role to monitor, facilitate and supervise. This includes school personnel, coaches, parents and youth pastors. Adults cannot direct student groups. It has to be student-led if the club wants to be a recognized school club structured similarly to all the other non-curricular school clubs.

However, if a Christian club wants to have more leadership from adults, it has a choice to not register as an Equal Access Act Student Club. Instead, the club can be structured as a Free Speech Student Club using the school facilities.

Is it better to form a Christian club as an Equal Access Club or as a Free Speech Club?

If students have the ability to lead a club, it may be wise to set the club up as a recognized student club under the Equal Access Act. Although the club must be initiated and run by the students, it may occasionally invite an outside speaker such as a youth pastor. It's best to rotate speakers and only invite them about once every four times to assure that the club is still student led. Also, youth pastors can meet with student leaders of the club outside of School and fully train them to run the club. Youth pastors often consider this an excellent opportunity for youth leadership training.

However, if students prefer to have more adult help or if they worry that they cannot maintain or grow the club without adult help, they may prefer to have the club operated as a Free Speech Club. This type of club is set up just like a community club, which meets in a school.

Christian clubs organized as Community clubs can be led by adults and even school personnel during after-school hours and inside the school.

(Elementary school cubs are formed this way as a Free Speech Club and are also called a community club.)

Does our Christian club need a faculty sponsor?

Many schools require a faculty sponsor for their "recognized student clubs" set up under the Equal Access Act. But the Act itself does not require sponsorship. Check out your school policy on student clubs. Sometimes you will find the policy listed on the school's or the school district's website, other times you have to request it. This faculty sponsor must be present in a non-participatory function only to maintain order. The teacher sponsor is present as a school employee and therefore cannot participate in religious views as this would violate the establishment clause of the First Amendment.

A Christian club set up as a Free Speech Club does not need a faculty sponsor.

Are students restricted in what they can talk about or do in their Christian club?

Students are fully permitted to talk about any religious subject. The school is not allowed to censor nor control the meeting in any form or fashion.

The school has to provide equal access to all clubs under both the Equal Access Act and the Free Speech Rights without regard to the content teaching of the club. Students can read the Bible, worship, sing, pray, preach and freely share the love of God.

Are guest speakers restricted in their presentations?

Guest speakers can also speak on any topic. Schools cannot regulate speech or exclude religious views. That would be considered viewpoint discrimination which violates the Free Speech Clause.

Chapter 11

TEACHER AND SCHOOL STAFF RIGHTS

Do teachers and coaches have free speech rights?

Yes, they do, but only among adults, not students. Teachers can freely talk to their coworkers about God. They can also have prayer meetings or Bible studies during free time with other teachers or school personnel.

However, in front of students, teachers can only talk objectively about God. Since teachers act on behalf of the government, an endorsement of religion would violate the Establishment Clause.

Courts have decided that the Establishment Clause overpowers the free speech clause for school personnel talking with students.

Can the teacher have a Bible on the desk?

A teacher cannot have a Bible or Christian book on the desk unless it is needed for an objective lesson on religion, nor can a teacher personally read the Bible while students are in the classroom. Teachers are considered agents of the state and therefore reading the Bible would violate the establishment clause. However, a teacher can keep a Bible inside the desk and read it when no students are present.

Can a teacher have a Bible as part of the classroom library?

The Bible can only be present when other religious texts such as Hindu, Jewish, or Muslim writings are available.

Can teachers wear religious clothing?

Unlike students, who enjoy comprehensive rights to wear Christian jewelry or clothing, teachers and staff are much more limited in their rights. Teachers cannot wear clothing with outright Christian messages.

The Christian Law Association advises that if a jewelry item can be purchased at a department store counter, it may be worn since its use would not then be limited to religious purposes. Many "rock" stars who are not Christians like to wear cross jewelry onstage, for instance.

May coaches pray with athletes before games?

No, coaches cannot pray with students before games or else it violates the establishment clause as coaches are considered agents of the state as well. Athletes may otherwise feel obligated to participate.

However, bear in mind that students have many more rights than school staff has. Students are more than welcome to organize a prayer before or after games. The key is that the prayer has to be student led. The coach may even be present at the prayer In a supervisory role to maintain order.

May teachers pray privately with students outside of class?

Teachers and students have to be outside of the school building to pray. But to meet students outside of school, parents have to be informed as well. Teachers have lost their jobs over this, so it may be better to just privately pray for the student. This holds true even if the student requests prayer.

Can teachers allow students to talk about religion in the classroom?

Yes, students can fully exercise their free speech rights in class as long as they respond to the topic at hand and don't interfere with classroom instruction.

Teachers should try to stay objective with their own opinion, but students are permitted to discuss their religious beliefs. However, all viewpoints should be equally encouraged.

Is there a way a teacher or coach can lead a Christian club?

School staff cannot lead an Equal Access club. School personnel are limited to a non-participating role. They can only be present to maintain order if the school requires teacher sponsors.[46]

However, First Amendment free speech community clubs do not impose that limit on teachers nor staff.

Barbara Wigg, for example, a third-grade teacher at Anderson elementary school has taught at five different elementary schools within the school district. She has participated in after-school programs for Girl Scouts and also taught private reading and guitar lessons. After she helped with a Christian club, she was challenged by a teacher which resulted in the principal trying to terminate her involvement. This is an interesting story you can read in the footnotes.

Ultimately the United States Court of Appeals, Eighth Circuit decided in the teacher's favor allowing her to stay involved with the Christian

---

[46] "Elementary teacher Barbara Wigg sued Sioux Falls School District 49-5 and Superintendent Dr. John Keegan (collectively referred to as "SFSD") to challenge SFSD's decision prohibiting her from participating in a Christian-based after-school program at schools in the school district. Wigg sought a preliminary injunction, a permanent injunction, declaratory relief, and damages claiming that SFSD's policy violated her First Amendment free speech rights. SFSD defended its decision on the grounds that Wigg's participation would subject SFSD to First Amendment Establishment Clause liability. Initially, the district court denied the temporary-injunction motion; however, the court later granted Wigg a permanent injunction after concluding that Wigg could participate in the after-school program at schools in the district-other than the one in which she taught-without raising Establishment Clause concerns for SFSD. The district court also ruled that SFSD's Establishment Clause concerns allowed it to prohibit Wigg's participation in the after-school program at her present school."
Retrievable at:
http://caselaw.findlaw.com/us-8th-circuit/1033214.html

club.[47]

[47] In October 2002, the Club requested access to SFSD's facilities to hold its meetings. SFSD granted the request, and the Club currently meets at five elementary schools within SFSD, including Anderson Elementary. The Club meets at Anderson Elementary from 3:00 p.m. to 4:00 p.m. at the end of the school day. Wigg attended the Club's first meeting in Anderson Elementary's library on December 15, 2002. Nine students attended that meeting, including some from Wigg's combined second- and third-grade class. At the meeting, the students played a game, learned a Bible verse, and heard a Christian story.

After the meeting, a staff member questioned whether Wigg could teach religion in the building. Noting staff use of the library at the end of the workday, the staff member expressed her concern to Anderson Elementary Principal Mary Peterson over Wigg teaching the Club in the library. Subsequently, Peterson informed Wigg that she could not participate in the Club meetings (which were held on school grounds) because of SFSD's concern that her participation in the organization might be perceived as an establishment of religion. Since that time, Wigg has not participated in the Club's meetings in any school within the district. Following her exchange with Peterson, Wigg sent a letter to Dr. Keegan asking for permission to participate in the Club. She informed Dr. Keegan that the Club requires every participating student to obtain a parental permission slip. The letter also suggested language for a disclaimer that would explain that any school district employees participating in the Club were acting as private citizens and did not represent SFSD in any manner. On January 17, 2003, SFSD affirmed its decision not to permit Wigg to participate because the school feared that allowing Wigg to participate in the Club would present Establishment Clause issues for SFSD…….

However, following is the court ruling from: United States Court of Appeals, Eighth Circuit.

With the guidance of Doe and Santa Fe, we conclude that Wigg's participation in the after-school Club constitutes private speech. Wigg's private speech does not put SFSD (Sioux Falls School District) at risk of violating the Establishment Clause: Wigg's speech did not occur during a school-sponsored event; she did not affiliate her views with SFSD (Wigg's counsel proposed a disclaimer explaining that any school district employees participating in the Club were acting as private citizens and did not represent SFSD in any manner); students participated in the meetings with parental consent; and nonparticipating students-unless supervised-exited the building before the meetings began. Under the inquiry provided in Santa Fe, no reasonable observer would perceive Wigg's private speech as a state endorsement of religion by SFSD. SFSD's desire to avoid the appearance of endorsing religion does not transform Wigg's private religious speech into a state action in violation of the Establishment Clause.5 Even private speech occurring at school-related functions is constitutionally protected, Chandler v.Siegelman, 230 F.3d 1313, 1317 (11th Cir.2000); therefore private speech occurring at non-school functions held on school grounds must necessarily be afforded those same protections.

We conclude that Wigg's participation in the after-school club constitutes private speech. Wigg's private speech does not put SFSD (Sioux falls school district) at risk of violating the establishment clause: Wigg's speech did not occur during a school-sponsored event; she did not affiliate her views with SFSD (Wigg's counsel proposed a disclaimer explaining that any school district employees participating in the club were acting as private citizens and did not represent SFSD in any manner); students participated in the meetings with parental consent; and nonparticipating students-unless supervised-exited the building before the meetings began.

Florida passed the "religious liberties act," in summer 2017 that mandates school staff "may not be prevented from participating in religious activities on school grounds initiated by students before or after the school day, provided these activities are voluntary and do not conflict with the employee's other assignments. School districts must give religious groups the same access to school facilities and ability to announce or advertise meetings as given to secular groups."

Other states have enacted similar laws recently to reiterate Christian rights. This helps teachers who are inundated with the secular agenda to realize that the Christian viewpoint is equally protected.

Can a school board member teach a Christian club?

In Good News/Good Sports Club vs. School District of the city of Ladue, the court held that a former school board member's involvement with a Christian club did not raise the perception of an establishment of

---

While we are aware that school districts like SFSD must tread carefully in a constitutional mine field of Establishment Clause, Free Speech Clause and Free Exercise Clause concerns, we reiterate that Establishment Clause cases stress the government's neutrality towards religion. Milford, 533 U.S. at 114, 121 S.Ct. 2093 (citing Rosenberger, 515 U.S. at 839, 115 S.Ct. 2510). Wigg seeks nothing more than to be treated like other private citizens who are allowed access to Club meetings. SFSD's policy permitting participation by all interested parties-so long as they are not district employees-in after-school, religious-based, non-school related activities violates that mandate of neutrality. As such, we affirm the district court's order allowing Wigg to participate in the Club at other SFSD school locations, but we reverse the court's decision prohibiting Wigg from participating at Anderson Elementary.

Retrievable at:

http://caselaw.findlaw.com/us-8th-circuit/1033214.html

religion.

The following section provides scenarios which could take place in schools.

What's the answer to the following situations?

Incident One:

Teacher Tony Richardson told another teacher she would pray for him after he disclosed some personal information. The two teachers knew each other outside of school as well since they attended the same church. However a few months later the two teachers had a fallout, and a complaint was filed against the teacher who offered prayer. School administration gave her a "coaching memorandum" which labeled statements such as "I will pray for you," and "you were in my prayers" as not acceptable stating she "may have imposed some strong religious/spiritual belief system" on the person.

Answer:

The school failed to differentiate between student and teacher. A teacher cannot pray for a student without violating the establishment clause. However, private talk between teachers, even on school premises falls under the free speech clause. When no students are around the teachers can pray or also have Bible study in school.

(This incident happened May 2. 2017 in Augusta, Maine)

Incident Two:

School counselor Jill Roberts invited Christian teachers to her office half an hour before school to pray for students. Teachers loved their prayer time and felt it make a huge difference in the school climate and individual student lives. However, another teacher with an atheistic belief complained to the principal and stated that the counselor was establishing a Christian program. The school promptly requested the counselor to stop prayer meetings. The Christian teachers decided to meet in an adjacent parking lot instead and prayed in the car. That worked well and ultimately that principal found the love of God later in life.

Answer:

The principal was afraid. Furthermore, he was not up to par with his knowledge of the law. The teachers had the right to pray in the counselor's office. They should have brought the teacher's guide to him (see appendix) to prove their rights. (This incident took place a few years ago in the Orange School District in Ohio.)

Where can I get more help?

The Christian Educators Association International (ceai.org) is an excellent resource for Christian teachers. It encourages, equips, and empowers educators according to Biblical principles helping to:

- Proclaim God's Word as the source of wisdom and knowledge
- Portray teaching as a God given calling and ministry
- Promote educational excellence as an expression of Christian commitment
- Preserve our Judeo-Christian heritage and values through education
- Promote the legal rights of Christians in public schools
- Provide a forum on educational issues with a Christian world view
- Partner with churches, parachurch organizations, educational institutions and parents
- Provide an alternative to teachers unions through resources and benefits including professional liability insurance and job action protection.

PART THREE

Elementary and Middle School Clubs

CHAPTER 12

THE POWER OF ELEMENTARY AND MIDDLE SCHOOL CLUBS

Do you know kids at school who need support and encouragement?

Would you like to see more of a Christian presence in the public school your children or grandchildren attend?

Do you drive by a school and would like to see a Christian club in that school?

Is God calling you to make a difference?

Would you like to bring hope and love to a specific area in town?

Intellectual Capacity For Faith Peaks During Elementary School Years

Overwhelmingly, research shows that the majority of people who become Christians come to Jesus while they are children. A series of studies about the age when people accepted Jesus as their Savior was conducted by George Barna, showing that people got saved at the following age:

32 percent of those between the ages of 5-12
4 percent of those between the ages of 13-18 and
6 percent of people 19 or older

In his book, "Transforming Children into Spiritual Champions,"[48] George states the following:[49]

> "Families, churches and para church ministries must recognize that the primary window of opportunity for effectively reaching people with the good news of Jesus' death and resurrection is during the pre-teen years. It is during those years that people develop their frames of reference for the remainder of their life – especially theologically and morally. Consistently explaining and modeling truth principles for young people is the most critical factor in their spiritual development."

> In light of this research, we have to ask very serious questions about whether the church is engaging in children's ministry enough. In most churches adults are engaged before children because they typically have more to offer the church as converts and potential leaders. Adults are positioned to lead congregations and have the resources necessary to help establish churches. Adults are certainly critical to establishing indigenous church leadership, but in light of the statistical information, and Jesus' own longing, we have to ask if we have put the proper emphasis on outreach to children and youth."

Intolerance of the Christian Faith in Public Schools

Moving up in grades results in public school students learning more and more secularism and evolution, which increasingly fosters doubt in God. With every passing year, students get more inoculated and hardened against God while they are immersed in the rhetoric of liberal teaching and atheism.

Jesus said that the kingdom consists of those who come to Him like children (Matthew 19:14)[50] and, though He was highlighting the posture of our hearts, the data shows that Jesus' words may have been

---

[48] Barna, George. Transforming Children into Spiritual Champions. Regal Books, Ventura, California (2003)
Retrievable at:
https://www.amazon.com/Transforming-Children-into-Spiritual-Champions-ebook/
[49] Barna Group, (2009). Evangelism is most effective among kids.
Retrievable at:
https://www.barna.com/research/evangelism-is-most-effective-among-kids/
[50] But Jesus said, "Let the little children come to Me, and do not forbid them; for such is the kingdom of heaven.

more literal than we would think because most of those who come to Jesus come as children.

Teaching young students can transform society because today's children are tomorrow's leaders. That's certainly a key strategy of the gay-straight Alliance Clubs which now exist in most of our nation's high schools teaching students that gender is fluid based on their personal preferences.

Shouldn't Christianity exercise those same rights? The motivation and drive of the LGBTQ community is stronger in our public schools than the Christian efforts. Maybe God has called you to intercept in your school and bring the love of God to students.

The Effectiveness Of Teaching Young People

If you can fathom the importance and effectiveness of teaching young people, you will make a huge impact in the lives of students. How many times have we heard that a teacher made all the difference? That "teacher" could be you.

High rates of divorce, dysfunctional families, the preoccupation of electronics, or just plain busyness of parents, leaves students vulnerable. Many of them will be spared of a difficult life because you showed them the love of God and pointed them in the right direction. More than that, you will be a catalyst for those students to live out their God-given destiny.

Why Not Embark On This Adventure?

Matthew 18:16 talks about little children or in our case, little students "At that time the disciples came to Jesus and asked, Who is the greatest in the kingdom of heaven? He called a little student and had him stand among them. And he said, I tell you the truth, unless you change and become like little children , you will never enter the kingdom of heaven. Therefore, whoever humbles himself like child is the greatest in the kingdom of heaven. And whoever welcomes a little child like this in my name welcomes me."

Matthew 19:13-14 "Then little children were brought to Him that He might put His hands on them and pray, but the disciples rebuked them.

But Jesus said: Let the little children come to Me, and do not forbid them; for of such is the kingdom of heaven."

The disciples rebuked those who brought children, but Jesus invited the children to come unto Him. Evidently their understanding is not limited, and the course of their life can still be impacted. This should be a major factor in how we approach children's ministry.

We must ask what Jesus wants of us? If we believe Jesus' words, then it's clear that He wants to reach them.

Matthew 18:10 "Take heed that you do not despise one of these little ones, for I say to you that in heaven their angels always see the face of My Father who is in heaven.

Jesus Admonishes Us To Teach Students

"Assuredly, I say to you, whoever does not receive the kingdom of God as a little child will by no means enter it." Mark 10:15

Elementary school students are the perfect age to learn about God. They are old enough to understand but young enough to still have faith. With children you don't have to knock down ten walls to get to the real person.

They are honest with others and themselves. Younger students are not yet overcome by hopelessness, doubt, cynicism, and anger towards God. Nor are they blinded by pride and sheer ambition. Young adults have a keen ability to evaluate faith and philosophy at deeper levels than adults.

CHAPTER 13

IT'S CLUB DAY...COME ALONG

The doorbell rings.

"Hey, Brittany come in. I'm so looking forward to the club today".

"Yeah, I'm wondering about the story though. It's a bit long but such a great story. I don't want to leave anything out."

"No worries," said Rachel "you know those kids love your stories. You make them come alive, and I usually see lots of awestruck faces. Oh, there is Mara pulling up. And Christine is right behind her."

"I love it when we all get together for a quick prayer and huddle before we head to the school. It's fun to ride to school together. And it's even more fun driving home when we get to laugh about all the things we could have done better," said Brittany.

"Mara are you doing that song with the movements again today?" said Rachel.

"Yes, and I also have two other ones prepared with movements, but I'll make sure the kids stay in their spot and don't run around the classroom. Can you guys participate in the action so the kids will get into it again?"

"Of course just like we can participate in eating the snacks," said Christine.

"Ha ha, actually you're lucky I brought enough along for you guys too. I made some fruit skewers. Kids like them," said Rachel. "Looks like we won't have any leftovers to bring to the school office then. I guess there's always the next time."

The four of them packed the lesson and game supplies along with the snacks in the trunk and got into the car.

The ride is always fun with lots of chatting and joking. The first step is the school office to sign in as volunteers. Sometimes we get to see some of our students in the hallway and make sure we wave and greet them.

"Hi ladies how are you doing today," the secretary said. As we get our visitor tags we hear on the intercom: "Today is Torch Club day. It meets in the library right after school."

That always makes us smile as we head up to the library ourselves to get things set up. The minute the kids come in, one or two of us try to stay by the library door to greet them.

"Hi JaQuan, Hi Allie"

"Hi Miss Michele"

"How was your day today?"

"It was okay, but Joey got on my nerves."

"Who is Joey?"

"He sits in class next to me, and we always hang out during recess but today he just walked away, and I couldn't find him. Back in the classroom, he wouldn't tell me where he was."

"That's not nice. I'm sorry that happened to you. Don't you wish you could just snap your fingers and make people do the right things? But we can't do that. We can only control how we react to it. But if we react in a certain way, we won't get hurt. Today's Bible story is about something like that. You know Jesus was rejected by many people, but then he always talked to his father God, who didn't reject him but loved him."

"Jesus was rejected too? I look forward to the Bible story today."

About fifteen to twenty students pour into the library where the club is meeting. This particular room has large tables, so we can have students sit at tables according to their grades to foster friendship building. When students get seated at their tables, the assigned leader engages in small talk while students write their name tags. Then the leader hands out snacks and fills out the attendance sheet to make sure everyone is accounted for.

"Alright kids, today's character education lesson is: Fairness," said Miss Michele

"What does somebody do when they're not fair?"

Renee said, "They laughed at the lunch I brought!"

"Someone pushed me for no reason," chimed in Ka'Isha.

"My best friend won't let me sit at her lunch table anymore," said Madison.

"Wow, I hear you," said Miss Michele. "Those kids are not fair. Let's watch this little video clip about fairness."

The 2 to 5 minutes video clip teaches students about how to be fair.

"Okay, so what have you learned about fairness from this clip?" asks Miss Michele.

"That we have classroom rules so there won't be chaos, " said Mitch.

"Yes, for sure, what else?"

"That we should be kind to others and not exclude them."

"You got it, Oliver. The Bible says to love your friends and neighbors just like you love yourself."

"Even as others treat us badly we should still do the right thing," said Kayla

"You nailed it. We don't have to drop to their level. We can be the better person. And then we feel better about ourselves too. Even if we don't agree with people, we should be good to them. That's what fairness means," said Miss Michele.

"Alright, it's time to get up for some fun songs," Mara said. "Let me show you the moves to the song again. And leaders, pay attention too. You don't want to do worse than the kids. Yes, you got it. Arms and legs this way. Ready to turn on music?"

Mara turned on some fun music on her phone which was streaming to a little Bluetooth speaker she brought along. Students are jumping, clapping, laughing, twisting and turning to the upbeat music. After three songs they're ready to sit down again to listen to the lesson.

Michele moved to the front of the room and said: "Hey kids why don't you come and huddle around me. Can you all see the pictures? Guess what the story is about today?"

Michele now teaches a faith-based lesson which highlights the character trait fairness: Zacchaeus the tax collector climbs the Sycamore tree to see Jesus.

She looks students in the eyes and tells the story in such a dramatic way that they feel like they're climbing the tree themselves. It's as if they sit in the tree just like Zacchaeus, who just like them, is too short to see over other people. It's like they're almost hiding in the tree when Jesus walks by. But he stops. He looks straight at them in the tree.....

The story builds more and more excitement......

As Michele wraps up the story, she focuses on applying it to their lives. For that, Michele moves from the story into the personal application without the students even noticing. It's all about them now and how they can learn from Zacchaeus and Jesus to do the right thing and make good decisions. She knows the personal application time is what helps students. Michele is constantly aware that this is about students and how we can help them navigate life and be sustained by the love of Jesus.

"How would you feel when you're up in the tree, and something like this is happening?"

"That would be so cool," said Ka'Isha.

"And then Jesus stopped right in front of the tree and looked up. Someone stops just for you, they notice you. What does that tell you?"

"It shows that Jesus knows and sees us and that He cares about us. And he's fair by talking to people who are not so popular too."

"Yes, Anna that's so right."

"Is that how other students feel when you stop to talk to them? Do you stop and listen to that intensely when your parents speak or when your brother and sisters speak? Do you want to do something about that? I know these are some difficult questions and you will need to think about them. We can talk about them next club time."

Miss Rachel moved into the middle of the classroom saying: "Here's what I want to do. How about some games?"

"Woo Hoo. Can we play the one from last time? That was so much fun," said Cara.

"I have an even better one for you this time. I brought two balloons blown up for you. A yellow and a blue one. The yellow one is for girls the blue one for boys. So, I need the girls to go on this side of the room," pointing to her left. "and I need the boys to go to that side of the room," said Miss Rachel. "Now, each group has to huddle together, and I will put a balloon in the air for each group. All you need to do is keep the balloon in the air. Whichever group keeps the balloon in the air longest wins. And the group who drops it to the floor first loses."

"Alright, ready set go."

After lots of jumping and laughing the girls end up winning. Of course, the boys want a rematch.

After that, it was time to move on to the next game. Miss Rachel gives each one of them a balloon to blow up and some strings to attach the balloon to their leg. The goal is to burst others' balloons and keep theirs intact.

Students are having such a fun time, laughing and enjoying themselves while making new friends. They don't want this to end, but they'll be back for sure next week for the Torch Club.

"Alright, the club is over. Hope you had lots of fun. Glad you came so let's pray before we part. What would you like us to pray for?"

"My mom is sick," said Caylee.

"My dad is in jail, and I wish I had a dad around," said Conner.

"I struggle in math," said Morgan.

Michele prays over the student requests. Then she prays a blessing over all the students. She prays for their school life and home life and demonstrates how beautiful it is to talk about a loving God. Next week she will ask about those prayer requests as the team has prayed over them all week long.

"Alright, I'll see you guys next week. I need those of you who walk home to the lineup along this wall, and I need those of you who will be picked up by your parents to the lineup on this wall," said Miss Michele.

One of the club leaders checkmarks the dismissal list for the students who walk home and walks them to the front door.

Another club leader walks the other students to the door and has their parents sign the dismissal list before taking their student home.

The other leaders come and mingle with the parents getting to know the families.

After cleaning up the room, returning the visitor tags and signing out at the office the team rides back home together.

"Did you see Julianne and how she paid attention? Her eyes got bigger and bigger during the story," Miss Mara noticed.

"I saw that. Her heart was touched. I was surprised by the good questions they asked afterward, too. It seems like they got it ", said Miss Rachel.

"Even Devin paid attention. And during prayer he wasn't fidgety," notices Miss Christine.

"We should just let them sometimes pray, too," said Miss Michele.

"Yeah, we can do a popcorn prayer. Whoever wants to say one sentence can. That would be a nice switch up. Let's try that next time," said Miss Rachel, "It feels so amazingly good to have shared the love of God with these kids and to teach them about fairness."

"I know. I feel like I did something life-changing today," said Miss Mara.

"Some of the students will always remember the story, or the fun songs and games or just even the love of God and how it felt," mentioned Miss Christine.

"I felt exhausted and invigorated at the same time," said Miss Michele.

"Tell me about it," said Miss Mara.

"This was our fourth Thursday. Club will be over in just two more classes,"said Miss Rachel.

CHAPTER 14

WHERE DO I START IN ESTABLISHING A CLUB?

Meet With The Principal?

Should you meet first with the principal to see if a Christian club can be established or should you find a potential volunteer/church first? That's really up to you. Ultimately you need to have both. Without volunteers, you cannot teach at the school, and without the approval of the principal, you won't be able to teach either. So I would go with what you have available. If you know a principal who is open to Christian views, then that would be a good starting point. Once that principal is onboard, you can then look for a church that is close by to help you with teaching. Or you can first find Christian parents/grandparents, etc. connected to the school who are interested in bringing God back into the school.

Recruit Club Leaders

On the other hand, you might want to talk to your church first. Is your pastor open? Definitely, the director of children's ministry should be contacted as well. You might be referred to the children's ministry team after discussing it with the pastor. But even if neither pastor nor the children's ministry director is interested, you can still talk to individual teachers or church members personally. Once you have an interested person, you can try to set up an appointment with the principal and take that person or the pastor along with you to the meeting.

Find Someone To Teach The Club

If you don't feel qualified to teach yourself, you need to find a teacher to teach the club. Either way, you will need a few people to help you manage the classroom. So you need to recruit either a teacher or a leader. The more, the better.

How Do I Find Help?

To impact the school of your children or grandchildren, you could try the following:

✓ Find other parents who are interested in establishing a Christian presence in the school.

✓ Ask your children to find the other Christian kids so you can contact their parents.

✓ If no parents are available, talk to your church about helping.

✓ Find out if there is a Moms in Prayer[51] at your school. Their vision is that every school is covered in prayer and they have prayer groups in many schools. One of those praying moms might help or know someone else. Either way, you should network with Moms in Prayer and let them know you're planning to start a Christian club. It might just be an answer to their prayer.

Do You Want To Reach A School In A Difficult Neighborhood

✓ Find a good church close to the school you want to reach.

✓ Visit the church on a Sunday morning to evaluate it and then approach the pastor to see if you can meet. Explain that their church is close to school and that many church kids most likely attend that school. See if you can interest those parents and church leadership to get involved in the school.

✓ Check with the school and find out if there is a church close by which helps with supplies or volunteers. That church might

---

[51] (2018) Our vision is that every school in the world would be covered with prayer. Retrievable at:
https://momsinprayer.org/who-we-are/our-mission/

already provide backpacks, coats or school supplies to help the school and would be the best church to also have a Christian club there.

✓ Be sure to check around before making a final selection.

Do You Want To Reach The School Closest To Your Church?

In that case, you need to motivate the following:

- Pastor
- Children's ministry director
- Children's ministry volunteers
- Church outreach team
- Your church friends
- Find out which church members have children attend that school and try to recruit them.

Recruit people for your team based on their interest. If someone likes to do crafts, do more crafts in the club. If someone loves to bake, bring great snacks. If someone loves music, let them do some worship. Whoever likes games, let them go for it. It helps to work with people when you find out where their strengths and interests are.

CHAPTER 15

CLUB APPROVAL BY THE PRINCIPAL AND HOW TO GET IT

How To Obtain A Meeting With The Principal

Principals are busy. It's not easy to obtain a meeting with the principal. Here are steps to take:

Find A parent

It's best to find a Christian parent whose child attends the school and then have that parent arrange a meeting with the principal. You can come along to the meeting and explain the club. Principals seldom turn parent meetings down. And hopefully that parent will be the one who helps you teach the Christian club. Even if not, it's a great blessing for a parent to arrange a meeting with the principal and endorse your plans.

Do Your Homework

If you can't find a parent, look for another Christian in the school such as a teacher, helper, cafeteria, office or maintenance staff, volunteer, or any person who can tell you how open the principal is toward faith. Just attend school functions and start talking to people. It's crucial to know where the principal stands faith-wise before any meeting takes place.

Secretaries are initial decision makers

Make the secretary your ally because she will decide whether you get a meeting with the principal or not. She can point you in the right direction with the principal, the assistant principal, the school counselor or some teacher who might be interested in character education or social emotional learning (which will be covered later in this book.)

Email
You can send an email to the principal. Principals' emails are readily available online straight on the school website. Of course, it's important to differentiate yourself in that email as principals are bombarded with, emails. Be sure to have a local connection right in the email subject line; something that catches their interest.

Follow up-call
Your chance of hearing back from the principal are not high. You need to follow up with a phone call and ask for a meeting. Because school secretaries are instructed to protect the principal's schedule, it will be difficult to get the meeting. You can also call after hours and hope that the principal is still there.

I don't mean to intimidate you about reaching the principal. Rather I'm trying to convey the importance of that meeting and that you only have one shot. Therefore it's best to do your homework and find out how open the principal is to a faith-based club and also how to best reach the principal. Once the secretary says no to you it's difficult to get through. And once the principal shoots you down you might never get another chance.

Meeting With The Principal

When you finally have a meeting scheduled with the principal, be fully prepared and have your documents with you. The principal has to have all the information to be able to make an informed decision right away. Chances are slim you will get another meeting.

Bring a sample of the permission form which would go out to the parents (see chapter on documents for elementary school). Explain the small print in that permission slip which reads:

The United States Constitution requires schools to respect the right of all external organizations to distribute flyers to students at school if the school permits any such organization to distribute flyers. Accordingly, the school cannot discriminate among groups wishing to distribute flyers at school and does not endorse the content of any flyer distributed at school. The school encourages parents to assist their children in making choices appropriate for them. This is not an activity of the school or the School District. The Torch Club is not liable in event of harm or injury to student.

Be sure to tell the principal that this is an efficient disclaimer for the school should any parent not like a Christian club. It clearly states that the school does not endorse the club and that there is no use for parents to complain because the law allows clubs including Christian clubs in schools.

Explain how you incorporate "character education" and "social emotional learning". Schools are mandated by most states to teach character education. Educational professional material is full of terms such as *grit,* which means to teach students perseverance. Schools appreciate help in those areas because they have to document how much the school teaches on character education and SEL (Social Emotional Learning). Familiarize yourself with this book's chapters on those topics.

Explain the faith-based part of the curriculum. Be upfront that this teaching will be backed up with faith-based stories. Mention that the Department of Education as well as the NEA and many other organizations support such Christian clubs. Principals are often surprised to find out how common these clubs are and that many schools have such clubs. Remind them of this being a voluntary club which is allowed to freely talk about God because a voluntary club cannot violate the Establishment Clause. Also remind principals that students, just like adults, have the rights to Free Speech.

Only talk about faith as much as necessary to honestly disclose the club's objectives. Principals get worried about atheists coming against the club even though the club is legal. Reassure the principal of the nondenominational nature of the club which will stay away from divisive doctrines. Principals need that commitment before letting you in a classroom. Remember you only have one chance, so be prepared and dress in business attire.

Invite the principal to attend the club. Also offer an invitation to the parents right in the flyer. Opening the club to them reduces their level of concern. I have rarely had parents attend and principals usually just observe for a few minutes.

Bring the filled out form called *Building Use Form.* Obtain a building use form from the School District Office before your meeting. If other clubs do not pay for use of the building you do not have to pay either. It would be helpful to find out if the other non-curricular clubs such as chess club have to pay so you can respond properly to the principal should payment come up in the meeting.

Offer a public information session. But only if the principal is worried about atheists who might oppose a Christian club. Instead of directly sending out the permission form you would first send out an invitation to an informational meeting about the club. Then you will see if opponents come to the meeting. When the principal sees that no opponents attend the meeting he/she will be more willing to take the next step of approving the club.
But the majority of parents will make their decision based on the permission form and will not attend a separate informational meeting. Be sure to include your telephone number or email on the permission form so that parents can call with questions. So again, an informational meeting is only recommended if a principal fears opposition.

This strategy worked wonderful in one of our school districts which was challenged by the ACLU about a Christian symbol. The school gave in and removed the Christian symbol even though they could have adopted the same symbol and language used at their State Department of Education. So the principal was worried about the school board and a Christian club. When he saw that no one objected to a Christian club at the informational meeting, he approved it right away.

Decide on a day and time right away. Ask the principal if certain days work for the school schedule. And find out what time school is out so you can start the club right after school. If you offer the club for just six weeks you might want to be in between school vacations so there is no interruption. Have a school calendar handy so you can make good supposition to the principal and have the dates approved right away.

School Counselor

School counselors are responsible for teaching character education and social emotional learning. They are typically open to having a community organization reinforce those character traits. School counselors can bring this social emotional learning opportunity to the attention of the principal and recommend your club.

We've had several school counselors call and inquire about the character education program. They love the program. In fact, one of the counselors in a Midwest city liked it so much she asked for over forty brochures so she could bring them along to the school district counselor's meeting. She told me later that not one brochure was left as every counselor picked one up.

If you know a school counselor who might be open for such faith-based character education, I would meet with that school counselor first before approaching the principal. The school counselor can further it with the principal by endorsing the club from a counselor perspective. Of course, if you do not have a connection to the school counselor, it's best to start with the principal.

In Summary

Be succinct in talking about the faith-based part. One time, a counselor wanted to see the faith-based part of our lessons. She then submitted it to her principal for approval who in turn denied the club because she saw a Bible story book. That's why we usually just mention that we use the most well-known Bible stories, but we only pull out the lesson if the principal requests it. Principals always worry about atheists even though we have constitutional rights to have a faith-based curriculum in a voluntary after-school club.

CHAPTER 16

CLUB MEETING OUTLINE

Attendance/Snacks: 10 minutes
Character Education: 10 minutes
Worship Songs: 5 minutes
Bible Story Time: 10 minutes
Bible Application: 10 minutes
Games or Crafts: 10 minutes
Prayer: 5 minutes

Sample club schedule for a sixty minute club

DETAILS ABOUT EACH ACTIVITY

Before Club

Club Leaders Should Be Ready to Greet Each Student.

This initial impression is one of the most important. Make each student feel special and welcomed. Greet the student and listen to what the student may be talking about. Guide the students to line up their backpacks and coats along the wall inside the classroom. This makes things so much easier. Then guide them to their assigned table. Have group tables according to grade levels. 1st grade, 2nd, 3rd, etc. Place a sign on each table which displays the grade for students to see.

It is important that leaders should never be preoccupied with private talk when students arrive, nor any time during class. The club teacher needs to set things up quickly since the classroom is in use until the very time the club starts. In order to assist him or her, the other club leaders need to do attendance, welcome students, offer snacks and create a quiet atmosphere ready for teaching.

Schools expect an orderly and quiet classroom. Students need to sense that expectation from the very time they enter the classroom. Yes, we want to have fun, but the minute you lose control of the class, you lose favor with the school administration and ultimately lose the club. Students can only have a good class experience if we prevent chaos. It is imperative to take control of the classroom from the get-go. Otherwise, the class will get out of hand. It's better to start out on the strict side. In a small class of ten students, this is much more easily achieved. The problem arises in big classes of twenty plus kids.

Begin

Let the fun begin. You need to be fair and fun so students will come back next week. Games, music, or crafts plus an exciting interactive story all make an interesting and fun class that students will love. The more planned activities, the better the result. Kids get unruly during downtime. Keep them busy and focused.

Kids mainly remember how you made them feel not what you taught. That's the most important factor to keep in mind. They will associate the goodness of God with the level of love displayed by your team! Making this a priority has great rewards.

Attendance and Snacks: 10 Minutes

Have students sit in small groups at tables while a leader takes attendance. This gives the main teacher time to set up the lesson, games, and music. While doing attendance have crayons or markers ready for each student to write a name tag. This will settle students down and will help you learn their names.

While someone does attendance, students can have a small healthy snack such as granola bars or animal crackers. Students are hungry after school. We do not recommend sugary drinks, maybe some water, but the food is more important to hold them over. If they drink too much during the class, you'll have more bathroom interruptions.

Character Education and Social Emotional Learning: 10 Minutes

This part of the meeting is where we as Christians can shine and offer great benefit to the public schools. It is called Character Education. (The use of this time is detailed in the forthcoming chapters called "Curriculum Options, Character Education, and Social Emotional Learning."

There are six pillars of Character in the Character Counts program. The pillars are: Fairness, respect, responsibility, caring, citizenship, trustworthiness. You can begin your teaching with any one of the six pillars. Pick one of them for each week as it ties in with your Bible story.

Worship Songs: 5 Minutes

Prepare the songs and have a mini speaker handy to play off your phone. Or, you can choose some. You Tube videos and play them on the smart board or via a projector you bring or even an Ipad or personal laptop computer if the group is small enough.

Many classrooms have blackboards called "smartboards" which you can write on. But they also have a double function and can serve as screens to show anything on the teacher's computer such as video clips or power point presentations. If you use the smart board, be sure not to change the teacher's cables. You can ask the teacher to get you into the internet on her computer, and from there you can show a clip or the Bible Images explained later in this book. But again, a better option is to use your own equipment.

Bible Story Time: 10 Minutes

If you have enough free space on the floor, you can direct students to sit on the floor for the Bible Story. This is especially helpful if you show printed visuals and students need to be close to see. If you use a larger screen such as the smart board, students can remain in their seats. If you do have room to huddle together, it's a nice change of pace and provides movement for those who learn through physical activity.

Use the visuals such as the power point presentation or printed Bible story book explained in the Curriculum Options chapter. If possible, display the visuals via the book, your projector or the smart board. You can bring a laptop or print out the pictures to show it to the students as you tell the story. Keep it interesting by speaking up and connecting with students.

Bible stories are a key component of the club. The objective in telling Bible stories to young students is not primarily for them to remember the details of the event, but rather to allow the narrative to reveal God's involvement in everyday life and to show the wonder and love of God.

Introduce the Bible story by asking a question, or showing a story-related household item that will catch students' attention. Use visual aids to illustrate story action. Conclude the story by linking the action of the main character to the lives of the students which will be the bridge to the Bible application part.

Bible Story Application: 10 Minutes

This is the time where you should break into small groups if you have enough staff. Being in a group of three to five people allows students to better express themselves and apply the lesson. Review questions will allow you to dig deep into the Bible story and apply the concepts to everyday life.

This is a prime opportunity to tie the Bible story to the student's world. Help them understand how God still answers prayers just like He did in the Bible story. Show that God can help just as much as He helped the Bible characters. Use questions about the story and connect to their personal life. With each question, you can steer students to real-life examples, so the Bible story comes alive.

Games/Crafts: 10 Minutes

The club meets at the end of a long school day, and we cannot stay strictly on the academic path. Students need a release and need to have fun. This is what keeps them coming back. You might have club leaders who prefer to do crafts instead or even do both. It's best to go with the interests and strengths of your team. If the kids have fun, they will come back and bring friends.

Prayer: 5 Minutes

Time often gets tight at the end of the club. Please don't underestimate the importance of prayer. Many kids have never heard a personal prayer and wouldn't know how to communicate with God unless you model it. Keep it personal so they feel included and be sure to use age-appropriate vocabulary when you pray. Remember, you are much more familiar with Bible terms and Christian buzzwords, so try to pray in a way they will easily understand.

CHAPTER 17

STEPS TO SET UP THE CLUB

Dates and Times of The Club

Discuss with the principal what day would be best to teach the club. The principal will know what other programs are running in the school and which days are good. It's best to offer the club for an hour right after-school one day a week. Of course, you could also offer the club for an hour each day after school for two weeks straight twice a year.

Start the club in late September or early October so teachers and students can get settled into the school year first. If you teach a six-week program, you might want to be done by Thanksgiving or Christmas. You can then start the club up again early in the year, like in late January or February before the outdoor sports programs interfere. Find out when Spring break is and squeeze it in before then, or right after. The principal might have specific time requirements. As long as it works for both of you and you can fit in the six weeks or whatever length you decide, it should work out.

Meet with the principal in summer before school or in November/ December for the club to start in the new year. Principals work through the summer, with just a few weeks off in the middle. You won't be able to get a meeting at the end nor beginning of the hectic school years. There will also not be any gatekeepers in summer, and you might be able to reach the principal easier.

Room Assignment

Principals are short on time. The more you get done in a meeting, the better. It helps to nail down the day, time, location, and how far ahead they want the permission forms sent out. An ideal room is where students can sit down at a table to have their snacks and do crafts.

But equally important is open space in the room where students can sit on the floor to listen to the story or play games such as circle games or musical chairs.

Another criterion is visibility to the lesson or media (this is important if you choose to use a projector). If the class is small enough, let's say up to 25 students, they can huddle together in a storybook reading setting where you show pictures of the story. However, if you prefer larger graphics, and especially if the class is large, you will have to consider using an overhead projector or the SmartBoard. In that case, your room would have to have these capabilities.

Classrooms are ideal. Newer school buildings have bathrooms attached to class rooms which prevent kids from wandering the halls.

Please keep in mind that classrooms are also the offices of teachers who need to prepare after school for the next day. However, it's just one day a week, and hopefully, a teacher will work with you if you choose their classroom. This is a sacrifice by the teacher and needs to be acknowledged.

We've had principals assign us to teacher lounges, libraries, gyms, and cafeterias.

- The library usually works well, but the librarian we had would have preferred her library quiet after a hectic day.
- The teacher lounge is not a good idea as teachers come in and out disrupting the class. Non-Christian teachers might not like to hear the faith-based stories.
- The gym works out ok, but students tend to want to run around.
- Cafeterias have worked out well for us in the past. Most workable are the ones which have and overhead projector. There's usually good seating plus open space for games.

Arrange for Parental Permission Forms

As we have discussed, permission forms are required so parents can choose whether they want their child to participate in a faith-based program. Otherwise, it would violate the Establishment Clause of the First Amendment. As you know, this clause states that religion cannot be mandatory for every student. You will find sample forms you can use in the Forms Chapter in this book.

Have your parental permission form ready when you meet with the principal. The procedure is that the principal will give all students an opportunity to learn about the Club and participate by sending their parents a permission slip with the information. When you meet with the principal initially, it is important to have the form ready.
This will be just a sample and will not have the exact date, time and room listed on it. But the principal needs to approve the permission form and can do that right away in that meeting.

Some principals may want to send it out at least four weeks ahead while others prefer two weeks. We've had some principals who sent it out four weeks ahead and then let us send out a reminder two days before the Club meeting. Some schools send physical forms home with the students. Others will send them out electronically. The same with reminders. For physical forms, you will need to find out how many students attend the school and then print out that many flyers with permission forms attached at the bottom to tear off and return to the classroom teacher.

Who Collects the Parental Permission Forms?

Either the secretary, community coordinator or counselor will collect the forms. The teacher will typically return the forms to the school secretary. In some schools the community coordinator or counselor will keep the forms for you. Find out who will do that at your school. If you keep everyone in the loop they will look out for your program.

Roster

Write up the roster once you collected all the parental permission forms. The roster will also serve as the attendance sheet. Students must be accounted for at all times. This roster needs to indicate if the student was present that day and how students will be released. It needs to contain columns showing if students will be picked up, take the school bus or walk home by themselves.

Once the roster is finished, the secretary needs it so she can let the individual teachers know which students need to be dismissed to the club. That's why it is best to have the roster categorized into grades. This is important because elementary students will not remember on their own to go to a club once a week. However, teachers usually dismiss students according to where they need to go. For example, the students who take the bus will be dismissed to the bus. And the students who walk will be dismissed to walk. The students who go to after-school care will be dismissed to that. And the students who go to the club will be dismissed to the club. You could have one or two volunteers in the hallways to pick up your club kids.

Dismissal Forms

You will also need to draw up dismissal forms for the parents to sign each time they pick up their child. This is a record to provide accountability that you have released the students to the right person.

CHAPTER 18

ELEMENTS OF A SUCCESSFUL PROGRAM

Before the Club

Be sure to get to the club twenty minutes early. It gives you time to sign into school, engage in small talk, and meet staff and teachers.

Leave extra permission forms with the secretary should parents request it. Also, keep extras with you at the club in case students want to bring their friends.

Club Announcement on the Public Address System

Elementary Schools typically dismiss students via the PA system and provide end of the day instructions. Be sure to find out if the principal or secretary make these announcements and be there in time every single time to remind them to include your club. Just seeing you before announcements jogs their memory. Have them announce the room you're in. It will remind the teachers and students that it's club day. At that age, teachers have to remind students to go to the club and send them to the right room. That is why it's important that you get to the club early.

Set Up

If the club meets in a classroom, there will be little time for setup. If the library has been assigned as your meeting room, you never know who or what group was using it before. Many times classes are held in the library as well. That's why it's very important to have everything ready to go and be organized so your materials and snacks can be pulled out in a minute.

Taking Attendance

Attendance is taken at the beginning of each class. With the climate in today's schools such as it is, it is absolutely vital to give an account where the students are at all times. That is why having more volunteers is helpful for you to run your club. Attendance needs to be taken at the beginning of each class. If a student is missing, that will need to be followed through. Your volunteer can help. While it may sound a little complicated at first, it will become second nature after you have done it a couple of times.

Here is how you do it. If a student is on the attendance roster but not present, you need to investigate. Ask other students if this student is sick and/or has been missing all day. Do not believe just one student as they can get confused. It is better to confirm it with two or three students. If classmates say that the missing student was in school that day, you should look for that student and then inform the office that the student is missing. It is better for you not to leave the room yourself. Send a volunteer. Sometimes students forget about the club and take the bus home or walk, but the school needs to be informed, and ultimately the parents do as well. At that point, either the school or you will have to call the parents.

Be Careful When Using The School's Technology

Teachers depend on their electronic devices to conduct their classes. Therefore, using their equipment is not advisable. This includes connecting HDMI cables to the overhead or using the classroom computer. It's too time-consuming plus too much can go wrong.

At best, you can ask the teacher to access the internet on their computer and show something directly from there such as the Bible stories: FreeBibleImages.org. Since the teacher's computer is already fully connected to and the overhead such as the smart board you should not encounter problems.

As an alternative and probably the best option, you can bring your laptop and a portable projector where you have everything preconnected and beam it onto a classroom wall or smart board.

One General Caveat: Talking About God In Front Of Teachers Or School Staff Is Not A Good Idea

Teachers take the separation of state and church very seriously. We are fully allowed to share the love of God in the club, but teachers are not used to that. Because teachers are restricted, they might be surprised to see us freely talk about God. Of course, we know we are allowed to share because we are teaching a voluntary club which meets after-school. But it's best not to talk about God in front of the teachers or engage in prayer. If teachers overhear it, you might want to explain the legality. It helps first to get to know that teacher to find out if they would have a problem with the faith-based teaching. Another reason to refrain from Christianese in front of teachers is that some can be offended.

Dismissal Procedures

Have the students line up along one wall in the classroom. Group those who will walk home in one section and the others along the other wall who will be picked up. Check the dismissal list to be sure they are really "walkers." Then have a club leader walk them to the front door in an orderly manner, which schools expect. Next, have the students who are picked up by their parents dismissed by walking them to the front door.

Students can only be dismissed to their parents or the names listed on the permission slip. Parents will wait for their students at the front door. One of your leaders will have parents sign out the students, and the others should use this time to personally connect with students and maintain order in the hallway. You will need to have a dismissal roster ready for parents to sign their children out.

If a parent is late, you will need to wait for the student to be picked up. Often, there is no one at the school at this time who could take care of that. For special circumstances, most schools have a community coordinator who can be called if a child is left behind. Have that person's number accessible. If necessary, the police can also be called to drive the student home. Although your heart may be in the right place, please know it is never advisable under any circumstance for you or your volunteers to take a child in their car. Unfortunately, there are too many legalities for this to be a viable solution.

You need to have the parents' telephone numbers with you at all times so you can make a call if someone happens to be late. Schools will give you back your permission sheets which contain all that information. Keep those with you for every class, so you have telephone numbers handy.

You have a wonderful opportunity to meet the parents at the end of the club. Although you might be tired at the end of the club, please don't pass up this chance to reach out to the parents. Find out where the parents stand and what they expect out of the program. Are they primarily interested in character education or are they also interested in the faith-based part of the program? Maybe they are concerned about their child's social-emotional well-being in school. They always like to know how their child is doing in the club, so feel free to share.

Parents will be interested to know If their kids are making new friends, fitting in and enjoying the club. This conversation can also show how you can pray for the family. You might even get a chance to invite them to church or answer any questions they have about that. Of course, to speak to the parents, you need to have enough people to help you keep kids quiet while they are waiting in the hallway for their parents to come. That's why your volunteers need to come to the front door for dismissal to greet the parents before they go back to the room to clean up. It's also a good time to further connect with students. There's always time for cleanup after the class because no one else needs the classroom then.

Tear Down at the End of the Club

Get chairs and tables back in order if you need to move them. Teachers figure out exactly where students should sit and since many chairs have pouches on the back with students' folders, it's important to have them returned to the same place.

Keep on good terms with the janitor. He or she is one of the few people still around during after-school hours. They are responsible for checking your room after your program. Please leave it clean.

Club Options:

Schools Offer Two Programs Which Can Incorporate Your club

If you don't want to have a standalone club and prefer to offer it in conjunction with an existing program, you can look at the following two options.

1. Enrichment Programs

Most schools offer enrichment programs such as art, chess club, science club, cooking, sports, etc. during a few weeks in the Fall and Spring. This is an ideal time to add a Christian club to that line up of activities. All those clubs require permission forms so parents are familiar with the process and can easily sign up for the Christian club. If you choose to offer your club during the enrichment program (or whatever the school calls it), you have to inquire what you need to submit for that.

2. After-School Care Programs

Most schools also offer after-school care for working parents. This program takes place at the same time that you teach your club. If you don't have that many sign-ups for your club, you can talk to the principal to see if those kids could be pulled out and join your club for an hour. The after-school programs are usually about three hours long. We have had it both ways. Some schools keep the program separate, and some schools allow the after-school programs kids attend.

If you are hesitant to recruit your own students when beginning a club, a good starting point is to begin with the after-school care program. In some schools, we just offer the club during the after-school program to only those students who attend that program. Logistically this is much easier. Students are already there, and you can have your club within that structure. Permission forms are still required so parents can choose whether they want a faith-based program. Otherwise, it would violate the Establishment Clause of the First Amendment. As you know, this clause states that religion cannot be mandatory for every student. And if after-school care students don't have a way to voluntarily sign up for this program, it would violate this clause. Therefore, the after-school program still needs to offer another nonfaith-based activity at the same time. After-school care programs are typically familiar with incorporating faith-based programs and will work with you.

The only problem is that the after-school programs are often restricted to a small percentage of the student body, and therefore the majority of the students miss out on the club if it's only offered during the after-school care program. However, it's a wonderful way to get started. After a semester or two, you can add the rest of the school.

Communication with After-School Care Program Coordinators and Leaders

The more you communicate, the better off everyone is. Even if you start with your own send along program, it will be good for you to introduce yourself to the after-school care coordinator or director, and even the leaders. It makes a huge difference if you tell them about the character education club and what you do. This will solve potential competition issues. It's also important to honor their program and become familiar with it. You will have a much better chance of them accepting your program which is the new program in the school and possibly coordinating students who are interested in both programs.

Communication Is Crucial

Maintain openness to tell everyone about the club whom God brings along. Schools have so many programs that it can be difficult for staff to keep up. Often teachers and staff were not aware of the programs that I taught after-school even though they all saw the flyer. After-school busyness prevents them from checking out clubs and programs. That's why it's so important that you tell them. Always have a sign-up form handy and bring it up in casual conversation. You could ask, "Are any of your students attending the Torch Club?" In most cases, teachers will say, "Oh, I teach music and I'm not aware of your program, but what's it about?" If you show them the flyer and permission form, they will remember and connect you with the club. Then the next time a student inquires about the club, they will usually promote it.

You may run into the classroom teacher who has heard about the Torch Club (or whatever name you have chosen) and even sends some kids to the club, but doesn't know what it is. You can explain that we provide character education using the six pillars of character along with some fun faith-based stories along with games and snacks. Once they know that the kids love it and have a good time they will talk much more positively about the club next time they get a chance. They might even encourage students to attend the club or even mention it to some of the parents at parent-teacher conferences. School staff likes to know about the new club and will appreciate if you take a minute to introduce yourself, to see who is teaching the club on the flyer they have seen. Be people oriented not just task oriented. Of course, this takes time. That's why you need enough club leaders to assist in building relationships. To this end, it is vital to come early. It's another way to ensure you're invited back for the next school year.

CHAPTER 19

CURRICULUM OPTIONS

For the Ten minute Character teaching in our suggested Club schedule, taking from a two part curriculum works best. The first part is any form of social-emotional learning which improves the school climate such as character education. The second part is the faith-based program.

Most states mandate character education. There are a few major programs accepted by schools. One of those programs is called Character.org and the other one Character Counts (charactercounts.org). Thousands of schools are using these secular programs, in addition to many organizations and corporations.

Most schools use either one of those two programs. It would be good to find out from the school counselor what program the school uses. Some schools have internally developed and written programs. If you find out the character traits the school reinforces, you will be able to incorporate it into your teaching. That provides a valuable service to the school as they can now document additional character education hours.

Why not use a Christian character education program? We want to provide a service to the school as well. It's wise to work with a program which is accepted by public schools. The character traits your particular school emphasizes is easily included in your Bible story. A principal may hesitate to allow a strictly Christian club to the school, but if it comes with a needed service to the school, it's easier to approve. Yes, the law is on our side, but principals can say no. Should that happen, the only recourse is to go through a lawyer. Since no one has time or money for that, it is better to find a need and fill it which will be more likely to guarantee your club's approval.

Character Counts listed below, for instance, consists of six character traits such as fairness. It's easy to put extra emphasis on that trait when you tell the Bible story. After all the whole Bible is about character.

Character Education Programs

Good Character

This is an excellent website used by many teachers and school counselors. It contains free teaching guides for elementary, middle and high schools.[52]

Character Counts

The character counts program focuses on six pillars of character:[53]

1. **Trustworthiness:** Being honest, sincere, forthright, and candid. Keeping promises. Being dependable and loyal.
2. **Respect:** Honoring the individual worth and dignity of others. Showing courtesy and civility. Avoiding actual or threatened violence.
3. **Responsibility:** Being accountable. Exercising control. Setting goals. Being self-reliant. Pursuing excellence. Being proactive, persistent, and reflective.
4. **Fairness:** Understanding the processes and results of decision-making through impartiality, thorough gathering of facts, and hearing all sides.
5. **Caring:** Being compassionate, kind, generous, and sharing.
6. **Citizenship:** Respecting the law. Doing one's share. Pursuing the common good. Protecting the environment. Respecting authority.[54]

---

[52] http://www.goodcharacter.com

[53] www.charactercounts.org

[54] (2018). The Guiding Power of Character Retrievable at: www.charactercounts.org

If you have a six-week program, you can incorporate one pillar or character trait each week. It can be presented via a classroom lesson (like you will find on goodhcaracter.com) or via a short video clip which is followed by a class discussion (see appendix) Each week the character trait is coupled with a Bible story which talks about that trait. The first week, for instance, covers trustworthiness. Then a Bible story on trustworthiness reinforces that teaching.

Character.org (formerly known as Character Education Partnership or CEP)

Character.org lists some organizations who offer character education materials.[55]

Faith-based Curriculum

One curriculum we have used is "Free Bible Images" at www.freebibleimages.org. It has amazing graphics for many Bible stories and is downloadable for free and can be printed or shown on a laptop. You can display it on the SmartBoard or via a projector on the wall. Many teachers print it out and have the students huddle together to hear the story. This way they can interact directly with the students and apply the lessons to their school and personal lives.

Of course, any children's ministry lessons would work. Parents signed up for this faith-based program and are approving of the faith-lesson. However, it's advisable to adjust the lessons to a school setting by eliminating doctrinal differences. You have little time to teach and need to utilize time to focus on the love of God. We have had parents complain and take their child out because they found out we are not Catholic which they thought we were. So be careful with doctrinal issues.

The same goes for handouts at the end of class. Keep in mind that this is not Sunday school. Parents can easily be miffed, or others who see the materials may oppose the club. We once sent a little Bible home, and since the King James Version is always on sale, we mistakenly picked that. The school office received complaints from parents. But they never

---

[55] (2018). Related organizations .
Retrievable at:
http://character.org/more-resources/other-helpfullinks/related-organizations/

terminated our club because we kept a good rapport with the school administration.

CHAPTER 20

CHARACTER EDUCATION

Character Education has been a capstone in schools for decades and is encouraged if not mandated by almost all states in the Union. Education Week reported in September of 2015 that the field of social-emotional learning and character education is "maturing and gathering interest from many corners of the education policy and philanthropy worlds."[56]

The Department of Education states:

> "Throughout history, character education has been the shared responsibility of parents, teachers and members of the community, who come together to support positive character development."[57]

Christian Clubs help with that responsibility by focusing on faith-based character education from Bible stories such as honesty, responsibility, caring, trustworthiness, fairness, citizenship, etc.

Many elementary school parents send their kids to our faith-based character education club so they can learn Christian morals and make friends. They might be too busy to bring their kids to church or don't really want to go to church themselves. However, they still value the Christian teaching and want their kids to learn about God and the Bible.

---

[56] Blad, E. (2015). Measuring Grit, Character Draw New Investments.
Retrievable at:
http://www.edweek.org/ew/articles/2015/09/30/measuring-grit-character-draw-new-investments.html
[57] Department of Education, (2018). Character Education: Our Shared Responsibility.
Retrievable at:
https://www2.ed.gov/admins/lead/character/brochure.html

According to Barna Research, eighty five percent of Christians find the love of God during elementary and middle school years. Faith peaks during those years before anti-Christian teaching puts doubts in their minds.

Benjamin Franklin stated: "… nothing is of more importance for the public than to form and train up youth in wisdom and virtue."[58]

"Education at its best should expand the mind and build character," [59]President, University of Carolina and former Secretary of US Department of Education: Margaret Spellings

"People grow through experience if they meet life honestly and courageously. This is how character is built."[60]
Eleanor Roosevelt

Theodore Roosevelt stated, "To educate a man in mind and not in morals is to educate a menace to society."[61]

What is character education?

Character education focuses on the social-emotional, ethical, and moral education of students. Numerous studies have supported the notion that students can only succeed academically when their social-emotional needs are met.

State and federal mandate to teach character education.

Not only have individual states mandated character education, but the federal government has also enacted character education. The United States Congress authorized the *Partnerships in Character Education Program* in 1994. *The No Child Left Behind Act* of 2001 renewed this tradition. The new *Every Child Succeeds Act (ESSA)* which was signed into law by Pres. Obama in December 2015 also contains language which supports character education via making sure that schools have a good school climate.

---

[58] Ibid

[59] Ibid

[60] Ibid

[61] ibid

How many schools teach character education?

Almost every school throughout the United States, be it an elementary, middle or high school has some sort of character education program. Those schools typically have ceremonies to recognize students or staff of outstanding character. Throughout the decades many good programs for character education have emerged.

What character traits are taught?

Character education includes traits such as respect, responsibility, fairness, caring, honesty and good citizenship. Teaching on those subjects improves not only student-student relations but also student-teacher relations, ultimately resulting in improved academic success.

How effective is character Education?

A study by Oregon State University researchers found that Positive Action®, a program which teaches social and emotional skills and character development to elementary school children, can improve academic test scores as much as 10% on national standardized math and reading tests.[62]

Other key findings include:
- 21% improvement on state reading tests
- 51% improvement on state math tests
- 70% fewer suspensions
- 15% less absenteeism

U.S. Department of Education Strategic plan: 2014 to 2018[63]

Following is one of the six goals of the strategic plan:
Goal Three Early Learning.
Improve the health, social-emotional, and cognitive outcomes for all children from birth through 3rd grade, so that all children, particularly those with high needs, are on track for graduating from high school

---

[62] Oregon State University, (2010). Research finds Positive Action® program improves students' test scores and behavior.
Retrievable at:
http://www.prweb.com/releases/2010/02/prweb3550744.htm
[63] U.S. Department of Education Strategic Plan for Fiscal Years 2014-2018.
Retrievable at:
https://www2.ed.gov/about/reports/strat/plan2014-18/strategic-plan.pdf

college- and career-ready..."

Following is an Example Of The Character Education Legislation for The State of Ohio[64]

> In 1990, the Ohio State Board of Education and Department of Education produced a document to assist schools in implementing character education activities. This document included character trait inventories, character education needs assessments, and sample lesson plans for the classroom. In 2002, H.C.R 28 (a concurrent resolution) urged the citizens of Ohio to encourage positive leadership and youth character qualities. It designated Ohio as a "State of Character" and requested that Congress take action to promote character education. Currently, Ohio Partners in Character Education (OPCE), with the Department of Education, facilitates character education programs in Ohio schools and communities and provides professional development, advocacy, a statewide character network, and the Ohio Schools of Character Awards. Current social studies academic content standards also include character education.

You will find the legislation of other states listed here:
http://character.org/key-topics/character-map/[65]

What is faith-based character education?

Faith-based education teaches the same pillars of character education such as trustworthiness, respect, honesty, citizenship, etc. To illustrate these concepts faith-based character education uses stories from the Bible since much of the Bible focuses on character. The Scriptures contain many stories about respect, honesty, integrity, and so forth. Bible stories are universally accepted by Christianity at-large no matter what denomination.

Character Counts

CHARACTER COUNTS! Is a program which teaches the six character

---

[64] Character Org., (2018). Character Education data by state.
Retrievable from
http://character.org/key-topics/character-map/#state-18393
[65] Character Org., (2018). Character Education Map.
Retrievable at
http://character.org/key-topics/character-map/

traits listed in the prior chapter and which have been accepted across all educational, political and religious spectrums for decades.[66]

---

[66] www.charactercounts.org

CHAPTER 21

SHARING THE LOVE OF GOD IN SCHOOLS

Sharing the Love of God in Schools

I often hear pastors and leadership teams express their interest to do something for their local school. Most of them quote the "separation of church and state" and believe they are restricted to provide backpacks, coats and school supplies. Many Christians lament about "when God took prayer out of school" instead of focusing on the huge opportunity to bring prayer back into schools. Clubs are a way we can bring prayer back and actually reach people who are interested—without pushing it on everyone and offending others, turning them further away from God.

When pastors find out that they are allowed to share about the love of God in their own neighborhood school, they are often surprised and delighted. These pastors encourage their children's ministry teams to get involved in their local schools. Many pastors prefer to be the teachers themselves and put together a team from the church. Christian clubs are excellent ways to make a difference in the lives of countless youth. The goal is the same as it is for Christian clubs in high schools to reach students with the love of God and encourage them to live out their faith. The only difference is that elementary kids can't do it all themselves; they need help, guidance, and role models. Elementary school students love to hear stories and really enjoy Bible stories. Seeing their wide eyes fascinated by the power of God is incredibly rewarding. Engaging in a conversation after the lesson is so powerful.

Calling All Parents, Grandparents, Church Leaders and

Concerned Citizens

No matter who you are, whether you're a parent, grandparent, or someone from the community, your participation can make a huge impact.

After every lesson, you will walk away energized and fulfilled knowing that you have reached young people with the love of God.

Proverbs 22:6 says, "Train up a child in the way he should go; even when he is old he will not depart from it." Perhaps the most important thing to remember about ministering to such a young age group is that whatever you teach will stick with them for life. Your words and actions will surely leave a lasting mark on every one of them. You can help set students on the right path before they might get into trouble.

These clubs are interactive, engaging, and a ton of fun for everyone involved - even the adults! The club provides a platform for elementary students to find other Christian friends and to bring classmates along.

Many parents want their kids to attend because of the character education or the social-emotional learning. Others are interested in the friendship building aspect. Whatever the reason, we have a wonderful opportunity to reach our young generation and bless them. What a privilege to be able to teach these kids about the love of Jesus and impact their lives as well as those of the whole family. You, too, can have a part in this awesome outreach, as a teacher or helper.

CHAPTER 22

SOCIAL-EMOTIONAL LEARNING

SEL is one of the latest trends in education. Educators are finding out that academic success is not necessarily guaranteeing a successful career. Students also need to be socially and emotionally up to par. Learning how to manage emotions and how to navigate social situations enables them to be better team players and move ahead in life.[67]

The professional journal for educators called Education Week[68] lists articles such as:

> Knowing how to control yourself and successfully resolve conflict comes in handy in the classroom, on the playground, and on the job. These skills are considered to be part of social-emotional learning or SEL, and leaders of a New York City-based nonprofit hope to share these lessons with thousands of students thanks to a $1 million grant. "We see the social-emotional skills as the essential foundation for success in higher education, in life, that you need to understand your strengths, [and] have positive relationships with others," said Laura Larimer, ExpandED Schools' senior development officer.
>
> SEL enables students to process emotions rationally. Some students come from families who respond to conflicts with emotional outbursts.

---

[67] (2013). What is Social Emotional Learning?
Retrievable at:
https://www.education.com/magazine/article/social-emotional-learning/
[68] Hinton, M. (2016). Nonprofit Receives $1M Grant to Help Support Social, Emotional Learning.
Retrievable at:
http://blogs.edweek.org/edweek/time_and_learning/2016/10/nonprofit_receives_1m_grant_to_help_support_social_emotional_learning.html?qs=social+emotional+learning

Those students need to learn in school how to deal more effectively with difficult situations.

Here are two more articles on how states are getting involved to improve SEL:

States to Partner on Social-Emotional Learning Standards

In a step that organizers call a "critical moment for the movement," eight states will work together to create social-emotional standards and plans to encourage schools to embrace teaching students about the growing field.

The Collaborative for Academic, Social, and Emotional Learning, which is also known as CASEL, announced the joint effort last month and will assist the states through consultation with its staff and a panel of experts.[69]

Organizers hope the effort will help school and district level educators deepen their emphasis on building students' social and relational skills in addition to traditional academic work.

States Preparing Expanded Toolkit in Assessment of School Quality[70]
Educators are still wrestling with what they should add to the mix to meet ESSA's mandate to go beyond just test scores.

The Every Student Succeeds Act gives states new responsibilities and wide latitude to rethink how they determine if a school is successful.

In addition to traditional accountability measures—English-language proficiency, graduation rates, and scores on state achievement tests— the new Federal education law requires states to incorporate at least one "other indicator" into their accountability systems. That indicator

[69] Blad, E. (2016) States to Partner on Social-Emotional Learning Standards.
Retrievable at:
http://www.edweek.org/ew/articles/2016/08/24/states-to-partner-on-social-emotional-learning-standards.html?qs=social+emotional+learning
[70] Blad, E. (2016). States Preparing Expanded Toolkit in Assessment of School Quality.
Retrievable at:
http://www.edweek.org/ew/articles/2017/01/04/states-preparing-expanded-toolkit-in-assessment-of.html?qs=social+emotional+learning

must be measured at the student level so that data can be disaggregated to show trends among groups of students, like racial groups and English-language learners. The law lists a few examples of "other indicators," including school climate and student engagement...

Some advocacy and interest groups have pushed for state leaders to use the new measure to dramatically reshape their education systems to include more "whole-child" factors, like measures of social-emotional learning, student support, and schools' ability to move the needle on student traits like grit and self-management.

Social Emotional Learning is an integral part of faith-based clubs. Lessons focus on the moral teachings of forgiveness, kindness, patience and self-control as well as fairness, honesty, trustworthiness, and many other similar character traits. Stories from the Bible encourage students to give their best and "love their neighbor", the ultimate commandment from God.

The Every Student Succeeds Act (ESSA) was signed by President Obama on December 10, 2015. Christian clubs can help meet the new ESSA mandate which requires schools to implement programs to keep up a good "school climate."

As mentioned earlier, it's good to communicate with the school counselor. Find out their current focus on Social Emotional Learning and/or Character Education and how you can support their teaching. We have coordinated Character Education Programs by using the school's terminology for character education reinforcement. We have also had schools adopt our character education program.

CHAPTER 23

DIFFICULT SITUATIONS WITH PRINCIPALS

What If the Principal Defers to The Superintendent?

A principal who is reluctant to approve the Christian club for fear of atheists might prefer this decision to be made by the superintendent. In that case, it's especially important to have documentation ready in a folder along with your contact information so the principal can provide this to the superintendent. In a smaller school district, you might be able to meet with the superintendent yourself. We have had a fear-based principal who wanted to cover all bases by asking for an informational meeting first and then deferring to the superintendent. Eventually, it was approved by the superintendent, and that school district now has clubs in several schools because the superintendent approved it for the whole school district.

What if the Principal Defers to the School Policy on Clubs?

School districts, as well as individual schools, vary in their policies. Be sure to research the school district website, not just the individual school website. School districts often post their policies on their website, or you can obtain them from their office.

What About School District Policies or Procedures?

Many school districts have established policies about school clubs and community organizations. One of our school districts has a roundtable of principals once a month who make the decision on outside speakers/organizations for the entire school district.

In that school district, we had to do a fifteen-minute presentation of our program to a roundtable of principals. We provided brochures, sample permission forms and a website in addition to a power point presentation.

After we were approved, it was easy to approach individual principals at schools.

Shall I First Talk to the Principal or School District?

Since the principal has to give the ultimate approval, it's best to start there. He/She will refer you to the school district if needed. However, it's always good to research the school district website first or even make a general call to find out what the policy is so you're more informed when you speak to the principal.

You need to be sure to show principals a copy of the Supreme Court case which allows Christian clubs in schools (see appendix). Remember to have to have all the other documents ready at all times since you will only get that one meeting with the principal.

The Lemon Test

It's unlikely that a principal will bring up the Lemon test[71], but for completeness sake and because it does come up in the church/state dialogue, I will mention it briefly. The Lemon test involves the Establishment Clause, and since students use either the Free Speech Clause or the Equal Access Act to open the door for clubs, the Lemon test does not apply to Christian clubs. It focuses on government funding of Christian programs and government endorsement of Christian messages. For instance, if an after-school program is offered by a church inside the school and receives government funding, the program is legal only if it meets a three- prong test originating from the legal case Lemon v. Kurtzman

For the after-school care to comply with the Establishment Clause, it must:

(1) have a secular purpose;
(2) have a predominantly secular effect; and
(3) not foster "excessive entanglement" between government and religion.

---

[71] http://caselaw.findlaw.com/us-supreme-court/403/602.html

In other words, the secular purpose is to provide child care, not Christian education. It's a faith-based organization which offers the same type of services a non faith-based organization would offer. In this case, the after-school care center would pass the lemon test.

However, as explained elsewhere in the book, we have worked well with after-school programs and incorporated Christian clubs. A Christian club is only a small part of the after-school program and not its main purpose. Also, the club is voluntary and cost-free, and students only attend if the parents sign up for the club. There has to be a parallel program offering for the kids whose parents don't want them to be in a Christian club.

CHAPTER 24

HOW TO COMPLY WITH SCHOOL POLICIES

School Facilities Use

Schools have a policy about the use of the school facility. It might be called: *Community Use of School Facilities* and is often simply referred to the *Use Policy*. This policy allows community organizations like churches, non-profit organizations, youth groups, and student-initiated groups to use its facilities to encourage the school's connection to their community.

The school might try and charge a rental fee for using a classroom, library, gym, or cafeteria as outlined in their Use Policy. However, if other clubs such as the chess club do not have to pay, then you would not have to pay either. Christian clubs should never have to pay a usage fee. Just be aware that some facilities managers and even some principals and administrators will try to levy a fee to help support the school. It's important to obtain a copy of the Use Policy before meeting with the principal if you choose to set up a club via the Free Speech Act as a community club. You should not have to pay and being informed helps.

Liability Insurance

Some Use Policies request the applicant to be part of a non-profit organization such as a church and to have liability insurance (which the church and most non-profits have as well). If liability insurance is requested, it's best to work via a church close to the school or via your church to be able to provide a copy of that insurance certificate to the school administration.

In the event you need to operate independently, look for an insurance company knowledgeable in nonprofit organizations such as United States Liability Insurance for nonprofits.[72] You can also talk to other clubs in the school who need insurance and can provide an insurance company referral.

Distributing Sign Up Forms

Some schools have an electronic bulletin board on their website and send out invitations to clubs electronically. Others request you to bring hard copies.

Visitor Procedures

Every visitor, including club leaders need to sign in at the main office. They will get a tag to identify them as approved visitors, which will need to be returned to the school when signing out. Be sure to tell your whole team to sign in at the front office.

Snacks

Some schools have guidelines for healthy snacks. Either way it's good to bring healthy snacks.

Teacher Sponsors

This is not needed for elementary schools. Only a high school Equal Access Club needs a teacher sponsor to guarantee order and safety. In elementary schools, parents sign up for the students to attend a club taught by adults anyhow who assure order.

Parental Pick Up of Students

Some schools allow parents to come in and wait inside the school entrance or in front of the classroom. Other Schools, although few, will not let parents come inside the school building after-school hours. In that case you will open the door for the parent to sign the dismissal

---

[72] http://usli.com/products/nonprofit

form and then dismiss the students into the parent's hands at the Front door.

School Regulations for After-school Hours

Most school administrators such as principal, assistant principal school counselor and even the secretary along with all the teachers are gone after school is over. Usually the maintenance crew is still around. And if the school has an after-school program then those after-school leaders are still in the school. However you are responsible for your own kids in your program. You cannot just drop them off there if the parents don't come to pick them up.

Parents Being Late to Pick Up Their Child

One of the most difficult situations to handle is when parents are late to pick up their child. It's important to always have your sign-up forms handy where telephone numbers are listed. Hopefully the parent has filled out more than one person who can pick up their child along with their telephone numbers. You should not take the child home yourself unless it is within walking distance. Inquire about school policies on that issue.

Community Coordinator

Most schools have a community coordinator who may be able to help with difficult cases where you are waiting for a child to be picked up. Be sure to get to know that person and meet that person early on. Hopefully you will get the cell phone number of that person so you can call if a child is not picked up. They might be able to have a family member to arrange and come and pick up the child.

In a worst case scenario, you will have to enlist the help of the police to bring the child home safely.

Exit Survey

Established programs use exit surveys to assure continued improvement of the program to evaluate how the students liked your program. These are typically done once after the course of your meetings concludes.

A Christian club offers an additional piece of the puzzle to improve school climate. Since schools are encouraged to measure the school's climate improvement, it would be wise for you to design exit surveys and submit those results to school administration.

Exit Surveys simply ask attending students questions such as:

Did the club help you learn about being a good friend?

Did you learn how to be honest, fair and caring?

Did you learn how to get along with others better?

Did you get to know others better?

Will you come back to the club next year?

If you submit the results of these questionnaires to the school administration, they would be able to include them into their own data collection.

At the elementary school age, you can conduct the survey by having students raise their hands to your questions and then tally those questions. Since parents pick up students, it's best to have parents fill out the questionnaire and find out how they like the program or what part they like best. This has been a great motivation for one of our principals when he saw in writing how much the parents liked the program.

The results of the surveys help principals and guidance counselors see the effectiveness of the club. Without feedback, your program might soon be forgotten. No matter how much parents like the club, they often do not take the time to meet with the principal to communicate this.

CHAPTER 25

AM I QUALIFIED TO TEACH?

Have you ever worked with children as a children's ministry leader, teacher or helper? Are you a parent, relative or love children? Is this something you want to do and are willing to prepare for?

Then you are qualified!

Are you a small group leader or Sunday school teacher? Do you homeschool or do you have experience teaching in general? Can you manage a classroom?

Then you will succeed.

It's the Lord who will go before you. He will prepare a way and show you. You can start small, by restricting the class size to a dozen kids or whatever you choose. But if God is touching your heart then you know He will enable you to do this. Though it may sound a little complicated when you are first familiarizing yourself with the rights and procedures to establish a club, it gets easier from there. Once you see the receptiveness in the children's faces, you will be glad you did. It's only one hour a week for six weeks in Fall and Winter.

Will you have the pain of success or the pain or regret? Either way is hard. God has poured this passion and gifting into you. Let Him help you bring it to pass. Ignite your calling and bear good fruit.

There is a cost to succeeding, but I believe it will enable you to do more and go even further. We are admonished in the Bible many times not to let fear stand in our way.

Jesus tells his followers twenty-one times to "not be afraid" or "not fear" or "have courage" or "take heart" or "be or good cheer". We need to push through our fear and let God empower us. He will be there for you and guide you with his wisdom.

Eccl. 5:7 says: "Dreaming instead of doing is foolishness and there is a ruin in the flood of empty words."

Use your passion and take the first step! God has equipped all of us with everything we need to do what He asks of us. It doesn't take a professional. Imagine the impact of scores of these clubs throughout our nation changing the future for children.

"Brothers and sisters, think of what you were when you were called. Not many of you were wise by human standards; not many were influential; not many were of noble birth. But God chose the foolish things of the world to shame the wise; God chose the weak things of the world to shame the strong. God chose the lowly things of this world and the despised things—and the things that are not—to nullify the things that are, so that no one may boast before him. It is because of him that you are in Christ Jesus, who has become for us wisdom from God—that is, our righteousness, holiness, and redemption." (1. For.1:26-30)

CHAPTER 26

HOW TO BUILD YOUR TEAM

Pray! Pray! Pray!

Ask God to show you and bring you to the right people. Always have a business card or brochure about your program with you. Many online companies offer printing and design assistance for these for less than $10. Share about the need for such a program in our public schools to see if it resonates with someone. Simply find out if someone has a heart for it. You'll find potential teachers in the following places:

Church

Get to know the children's ministry team. Talk to them about reaching children in schools. First, talk to the children's ministry director to see if there's any interest. Even if the director doesn't have any interest, you might well find a children's ministry leader who wants to reach our local schools.

School

If you are a parent of a student, you have the optimal opportunity to find other Christian parents when you attend ball games or school events. Plant the thought in their mind that it would be wonderful for the Christian children to get together. What better place than to have a Christian club. You'd be surprised how many mothers would want to be involved themselves.

Women's Groups and Bible Studies

It does not have to be just your own Bible study. You can find out about Bible studies in the church and ask if you could share five minutes. You're not asking for money, so this is very easy to do. They will want to hear what you are saying because you are talking about their school kids and how to help them.

Women's Conferences

At a woman's conference, you can ask to set up a table and talk about the school program. Or you can ask if you can share from the pulpit for five minutes about the opportunity to bring the love of God into our public schools.

Church Administration

Speak to the pastor about this opportunity. If the pastor likes the idea and agrees to it, he might endorse you to the children's pastor who then will be much more open towards helping you. Usually, the larger the church, the more difficult it is to get a meeting with the pastor. But don't lose heart. Pastors are constantly getting bombarded with many ministry ideas. If the pastor is not open or the church is too big you may be able to talk to an assistant pastor or secretary or to whomever the Lord guides you.

Children's Ministry Pastor

Even though it's ideal if the senior pastor first endorses it, it is not an absolute requirement. If the children's ministry pastor is catching the vision, that's all it takes. He or she may get involved personally and/or help recruit a team.

Youth Pastor

The youth pastor is vital to contact when attempting to get into high school. I even suggest contact for middle school clubs as well. Usually, this minister is a young, fun, dynamic person. He or she may not only send kids your way, but be able to speak once a month as was mentioned earlier. Even if you are only concentrating on a club in elementary school, it's still good to talk to the youth pastor because he/she might want to talk with his/her Youth leadership team to help out. Teenagers can help manage the classroom just like they often help in the children's department in church.

Grandparents and Older People

Elementary school children respond well to loving grandma and grandpas. That's the great part about an elementary school program - anyone at any age can help - from teenagers to people well into their seventies. Remember, all you need to have is one good teacher, and the other people are just helping with classroom management. Don't overlook the student's grandparents as they are perfect candidates for such a ministry.

Other Churches

If you can't find enough people from your church, look around your neighborhood and see if there's another church close to the school you are selecting. Attend one of their functions and start talking about reaching the school to whomever the Lord brings in your path.

Bulletin Insert

Ask the communication person in your church about a school ministry insert into the bulletin.

ELEMENTARY SCHOOL DOCUMENTS

SAMPLE PERMISSION FORM FOR ELEMENTARY SCHOOLS

Hey Kids!! Come and join the amazing Torch Club!

What? We play games, make friends, learn character education, hear amazing faith-based stories, sing fun songs, have snacks and just have fun! Students will learn the six pillars of character: Trustworthiness, respect, responsibility, fairness, caring, and citizenship. We search for the gold in students and focus on instilling self-worth and identity.

When? Tuesdays March 29 - May 3 After school till 3:15
Where? Schreiber School (K-2)
Teacher? Linda Zimmer, Gingrich Myers

Parents are welcome to observe or stay. There is no cost for the nondenominational Torch Club. We stay away from doctrinal differences as we focus on uniting themes such as the love of God.

The United States Constitution requires schools to respect the right of all external organizations to distribute flyers to students at school if the school permits any such organization to distribute flyers. Accordingly, the school cannot discriminate among groups wishing to distribute flyers at school and does not endorse the content of any flyer distributed at school. The school encourages parents to assist their children in making choices appropriate for them. This is not an activity of the school or the School District. The Torch Club is not liable in event of harm or injury to student.

Torch Club Sign-up! Please return right away!

First Name:
Last Name:

Age:
Grade:
Address:

Phone:
Medical Conditions:

Parent Name:
Permission to take pictures of class: Yes   No

Emergency Contact:

Who can pick up my child:

My child will be: Picked up   Walk home

Would you like a clean copy to take to meetings?
Go to: http://partnerwithschools.org/resources.html

CHAPTER 28

SAMPLE LEADER APPLICATION

Leader Application

Thank you for your interest in volunteering and bringing the love of God back into our public schools. We have a policy that states volunteers must be of an exemplary godly character and display it in their life style. Thank you for completing the following questions with your signature and date.

Name:Middle I.
DOB:
Address:
Cell Phone:
E-Mail:
Occupation:
Employer:
Home Phone:
Years of Education
Bible or other training (writing, graphic arts, computers, outreach, teaching, networking, etc.):

Briefly describe your "born again" experience?

List any Christian work in which you have engaged:

Why do you want to volunteer?

Home Church Name:
Pastor:
Phone:
Please list two people we can contact for references (not family):
Name:
Relationship:
Phone:
Name:
Relationship:
Phone:
I verify that the above information is true and accurate to the best of my knowledge. I authorize the club leader to contact the above references and to conduct a background check. Background checks are mandatory for staff and volunteers in public schools.

Signature
Date:
Social Security Number
Social Security Number along with the correct birth date and full name are needed for the background check. Background checks are for criminal and sex offenses not for traffic tickets or childhood misdemeanors.

Would you like a clean copy to take to meetings?
Go to: http://partnerwithschools.org/resources.html

CHAPTER 29

SAFETY POLICY AND BACKGROUND CHECK

Safety Policy Manual

Any adult who interacts with students in a school setting has to become familiar with student safety. As the club leader, you need to make sure that you have a safety policy which explains procedure to assure physical and sexual safety. Sexual predators tend to want to become volunteers for children's organizations. You can find a sample policy on our website:

http://partnerwithschools.org/resources.html[73]

Feel free to copy that policy for your purposes. Be sure to thoroughly go over this policy with each volunteer and have them sign it. In today's legal climate, this will be required by any insurance and will help protect you should something happen.

Background Check

In addition to having volunteers sign a safety policy, you will need to obtain a background check. Most churches routinely run background checks on their children's volunteers, so you can ask your volunteer to request a copy from church. Or you could ask your church if they would run a background check for you and your volunteers.

Of course, you can run them yourself on the internet for about $25 as

---

[73] www.partnerwithschools.org

well. Background USA[74] is one of such companies. To run a background check, all you need to have is written permission from the person you are checking. This is why the volunteer application has that request included.

---

[74] https://www.backgroundsusa.com

CHAPTER 30

SUPREME COURT ALLOWS CHRISTIAN CLUBS

Following is an ABC News article about the Supreme Court rendering of Christian clubs in public school. This is the current precedent case which endorses Christian clubs.

Supreme Court Says Religious Clubs Can Meet at Public Schools
By Anne Gearan
Washington, June 11, 2001

The Supreme Court ruled for a Christian youth group today in a church-state battle over whether religious groups must be allowed to meet in public schools after class hours.

In a 6-3 decision that lowered the figurative wall of separation between church and state, the justices said a New York public school district must let the Good News Club hold after-school meetings for grade-school children to pray and study the Bible.

Justice Stephen Breyer, usually a moderate-to-liberal vote on the court, joined the five most conservative members in partial support of the religious club's request. Justices John Paul Stevens, Ruth Bader Ginsburg and David Souter dissented.

The majority found that excluding the club was unconstitutional discrimination based on the club's views. Letting the meeting take place would not be an unconstitutional government endorsement of religion, the court ruled.

The Constitution's First Amendment protects free speech and the free exercise of religion, but it also bars government establishment of religion.

Christianity Over Other Religions?

The Milford School District in upstate New York had argued that allowing the Good News Club to hold what school officials called "the equivalent of religious worship" at the school would amount to a school endorsement of Christianity over other religions.

The Good News Club said the school was discriminating against it based on its views.

The youth group's members range from age 5 to 12, and its meetings include Bible stories, prayers and teaching children to "give God first place in your life." The club has met at a local church since the school denied its 1996 request to use the school building after 3 p.m. on school days.

A Contentious Issue

The Supreme Court has long wrangled with the question of religion in the public schools. The justices banned organized prayer during class hours in the early 1960s, and in the past decade banned clergy-led prayer at high school graduation ceremonies and student-led prayer at high school football games.

But the court also ruled in 1993 that a New York public school must let a religious group use its building to show Christian movies during evening hours.

In cases involving the use of public money for church-run schools, the justices allowed taxpayer-funded computers and remedial help by public school teachers at religious schools.

The Milford school has had a policy since 1992 allowing community use of its building after class hours for "social, civic and recreational meetings" and other uses for the community's welfare. The Boy Scouts, Girl Scouts, and 4-H Club are among the groups that have met at the school.

The school district's lawyers contended that because the Good News Club's members were grade-school age and the meetings would be held immediately after school, some children might be confused into believing the school district endorsed the club's religious message.

Allegations of Discrimination

The Good News Club contended the school was discriminating against it while allowing other groups such as the Boy Scouts to teach moral values at the school building. A federal judge and the 2nd U.S. Circuit Court of Appeals upheld the school district's policy.

Today, the Supreme Court reversed that decision and sent the case back to the lower court.

By letting other groups use the school after hours, school officials created a public forum, the court found.

"When Milford denied the Good News Club access to the school's limited public forum on the ground that the club was religious in nature, it discriminated against the club because of its religious viewpoint in violation of the free-speech clause of the First Amendment," Justice Clarence Thomas wrote for the majority
The case is The Good News Club v. Milford Central Schools, 99-2036.

Would you like a clean copy to take to meetings?
Go to: http://partnerwithschools.org/resources.html

PART FOUR

High School Clubs

CHAPTER 31

WHAT TO DO FIRST

"Mom, Jake is in pain," Zack's voice was tense on the phone.

"Can you come help? We're at the skate park by the school. Hurry!"

Amy grabbed her keys, not sure what to do. Her mind was racing as much as the car, wondering why his parents didn't help and what else the boys were into.

"I can't stand on my leg. My ankle hurts like crazy."

"Ok, Zack. Help me carry him to the car."

While his doctors looked at Jake's ankle, mom talked to Zack about his friends. She was worried about more than broken bones.

"He's a great friend mom. What do you want? I know you'd like me to hang out with other Christians, but they're hard to find in school. I have to take what I get."

Find Strength and Connection in A Christian Atmosphere

Students like Zack would benefit from a Christian community in school where they can find like-minded friends.

High School Christian clubs provide an oasis for Christian students who live in a religiously pluralistic society steeped in secular teaching. Foremost, Bible clubs should be a venue for Christian students to find each other and form friendships to help survive in an anti-Christian environment. Students are vulnerable and impressionable during those formative years and need support.

Investigate

Most High Schools already have a Christian club. Why not find other Christians and get into that huddle? Don't start your club without learning the lay of the land. See if you can get involved and support that club.

The subsequent chapters show you how to find other Christian students and staff. You will learn how to approach them and obtain the information they have gathered over the years. Someone in the school knows where the principal stands on faith issues, and it's wise to find that person.

Find out if another Christian club or the Fellowship of Christian Athletes (FCA) exist. If the school only has a club for Christian athletes you might consider starting one for other students as well. Keep in mind that FCA also helps set up a non-athletic club called the Fellowship of Christians. Since the school has already approved FCA, you could consider this one because it will be approved easily. You will find other organizations listed in this chapter equally good and may suit you better.

Either way, you need to find out which Christian clubs currently operate at your school and what happened in the past if a former Christian club is no longer active.

Research Organizations Which Help Build Christian Clubs

At the high school level, you have lots of help to set up or strengthen a club. The Cru organization, for instance, has a coaching program where you will be coached for free through the whole process. Others do the same. They will also have a strategic plan on how to set up and grow a club. But you must request that plan. Most organizations don't have them on their website but make them available if asked. No need to do this alone when someone can show you the way and warn you of pitfalls.

Following organizations can be of help:

Cru

http://www.cruhighschool.com

Youth for Christ
http://www.yfc.net

Young Life
http://Younglife.org

Fellowship of Christian Athletes
http://www.fca.org

Those organizations also have multiple other materials to help you.

Get Your Church Involved

Prayer Partners
You need all the prayer you can get because you are entering secular territory. That is not popular with our adversary who would like to think the children are his. Talk to your pastor early in the process so you feel supported and they are a part of owning the vision. Also, talk to your youth pastor and church prayer team. It's wise to keep these key church leaders continually updated. Don't just stop after the initial meeting.

Youth Pastor Advice
A youth pastor knows exactly how to grow a youth group. Tap into that expertise. Try to meet every week or two to get help with furthering your mission. Bring your club leadership along. The more mentoring you receive the less you will get derailed.

Next Steps

The following chapters will explain the Equal Access Act and the First Amendment Rights. It will explain the difference between the two as you can set up clubs using either one of those legal rights. It gets a bit tricky but hang in there. Dialogue chapters make it easier to understand. For the studious, the legal text is provided at the end.

- ✓ You will receive step by step instruction on setting up a club.
- ✓ You will learn exactly how to speak with a principal and even educate that principal on your rights in case they oppose.
- ✓ This section includes a chapter on Gay-Straight Alliances

because most high schools have those clubs now. It will prepare you to prevent potential clashes.

✓ You will also be prepared to communicate with atheists since the majority of Gay- Straight Alliance club members are atheists as well.

Get ready for an amazing adventure. If you're a high school student it will bring you closer to God, help you find life long friends and looks amazing on any resume!

And if you're a pastor, youth leader, or parent, you'll know that many student lives will be impacted by whole families attending church.

CHAPTER 32

THE EQUAL ACCESS ACT

Students have two options to establish meetings on school campus:

a) They can use the First Amendment Free Speech rights as explained throughout this book so far. Those rights apply to all K-12 schools.

b) Or, they can use the Equal Access Act as explained in the following story with Chloe. However, the Equal Access Act applies only to Secondary Schools. High Schools are always secondary schools. But each state decides if middle schools are included as secondary schools.

Up to the year 1984, all Christian clubs were established via the Free Speech Rights. However, when mandatory prayer was taken out of schools, many school officials thought that all of the religion should be banned. This led to discrimination against religious clubs and ultimately resulted in the United States Congress introducing and passing the Equal Access Act.

The Act states that if a secondary public school receives Federal funds and has a limited open forum, it must provide equal access to all non-curricular clubs during non-instructional time. Schools cannot prohibit such clubs unless they "materially and substantially interfere with the orderly conduct of educational activities within the school."[75]

---

[75] Many state constitutions have establishment clause provisions that are more restrictive than the First Amendment. In some such instances, state law bars all religious meetings on public school grounds and thus comes into direct conflict with the EAA. One appellate court found that, when these conflicts arise, the EAA preempts (overrules) the state law. Garnett v. Renton, 987 F. 2d 641 (9th Cir.), cert. denied, 510 U. S. 819 (1993).

The Equal Access Act Consists of Three Parts

1. Nondiscrimination
Schools cannot discriminate "on the basis of religious, political, philosophical, or other content of the speech at such meetings"

2. Student-Initiated
If a Christian club decides to use the Equal Access Act as the legal way to establish the club it must not only be student initiated but also student-led.

3. School Control
Schools are only allowed to restrict the club to maintain order and to protect the safety and well-being of students and faculty. However, school officials do have the right to entirely shut down all non-curricular clubs. Prohibiting every single club including the football team would constitute closing the limited open forum, and the Equal Access Act would no longer apply to require equal access to all clubs.

What Does Equal Access Mean?
The school has to provide equal access to all non-curricular clubs. If one or more curricular clubs exist, the school has established a limited open forum, and must provide equal access to all facilities to the clubs such as: classrooms, copy machines, intercoms, club fairs, bulletin boards, school newspapers, yearbook pictures or any other benefit provided to a secular club.[76]

What Is A Secondary School?
State law, not federal law, defines which grades are considered secondary schools. Grades 9-12 are always included. Middle school classification varies by state.

In recent years, the Gay-Straight Alliance established numerous GSA[77]

Retrievable at:
http://archive.adl.org/religion_ps_2004/clubs.html
[76] Staver, Eternal Vigilance, 2005, p. 119
[77] (2013) Can and Should Middle Schools Allow Gay-Straight Alliances?
Retrievable at:

Clubs nationwide. Those clubs are based on the Equal Access Act which requires the middle school to be labeled a secondary school by each state.

What Is A Student-Initiated Club?

The club has to be started and controlled by students not adults. Neither school employees nor outside people can initiate or maintain the club. Students can invite outside speakers, but those speakers cannot be regulars or come more often than every three or four meetings. However, students can meet as often as they want with a mentor outside of school who helps and instructs them on how to successfully run a club. Students may choose their club leaders restricting certain leadership roles to their beliefs. "However, general membership probably cannot be limited."[78]

What Is A Non-Curricular Club?

The Supreme Court stated that a non-curricular club is *any student group that does not directly relate to the body of courses offered by the school*.[79] For example chess clubs, drama clubs and community service clubs, etc. fall into that category.

What Is Non-Instructional Time?

Non-instructional time[80] is any time when no instruction takes place. It includes the morning before classroom instruction begins or in the afternoon when the instruction is over. Lunches and free periods are also considered non-instructional time. If other clubs are meeting during certain times, the Christian club has the same privilege.

Can the School Deny a Christian Club If The School Has Not Created A "Limited Open Forum"?

Yes. Any club using the Equal Access Act can only be started if the

---

[78] (2018) Student-Initiated Religious Clubs. Retrievable at:
https://www.adl.org/education/resources/tools-and-strategies/religion-in-public-schools/clubs
[79] (1990) Board of Educ. v. Mergens, 496 U.S. 226
Retrievable at:
https://supreme.justia.com/cases/federal/us/496/226/case.html
[80] Hsu v. Roslyn Union Free School. Dist., 85 F. 3d 839 (2nd Cir.), cert. denied, 519 U. S. 1040 (1996).

school board has a policy to agree to have a limited open forum. If at least one other non-curricular club exists in the school, the school has already created a limited open forum and needs to allow the Christian club as well.

However, a Christian club can also be established in this case via the First Amendment Rights which does not need a limited open forum.

Can A School Regulate When And Where The Club Meets?

The school has the authority to set a reasonable time and place. However it must not discriminate and must apply those guidelines to all clubs equally.

Do I Need A Teacher Sponsor for The Club?

The Equal Access Act does not mandate school sponsors. Therefore, sponsorship is determined by individual school policies. If the school does require club sponsors it's important to know that sponsors of other clubs are allowed to be active participants in the club. However, the act stipulates that the sponsors of Christian clubs can only attend in a non-participatory function. This is to prevent the appearance that the school is trying to establish religion and violate the establishment clause.

Can Students Disseminate Flyers About Their Club or Announce the Club Meeting On The Intercom?

Yes, Christian clubs have the same rights as other clubs to promote and invite other students to the club. This does not constitute an official endorsement by the school which would violate the establishment clause.

What If the School Is Fearful of Violating the Establishment Clause?

Even though the Mergens case mentioned below ruled that a Christian club does not violate the establishment clause, some school officials are still fearful. They may balk when students exercise their right to send out flyers or make an announcement on the intercom. The best solution is to provide them information that is allowed.

If schools want to avoid the appearance of a possible establishment violation they can add a disclaimer to the bottom of the flyer or at the end of the announcement stating that this activity is not officially endorsed by the school. (See sample form in this book)

Can Outside Speakers or Community Leaders Speak at Meetings?

Non-students *may not direct, conduct, control, or regularly attend activities of student groups.*[81] Speakers may infrequently come to meetings if invited by the students and if the school does not prohibit such guests in other clubs. However, school administration is allowed to prohibit outside speakers in a Christian club if they prohibit speakers in all of the school's non-curricular school clubs.[82]

Board Of Education v Mergens: A Supreme Court Case

Bridget Mergens,[83] a student from Westside High School, wanted to establish a Christian club in her school. Her school received federal funds and offered some other voluntary clubs during non-instructional time.

However, school officials denied Bridget's request, citing the establishment clause and the fact that the club had no faculty sponsor despite the fact that the school refused to allow a faculty sponsor. The issue was then brought before the school board which resulted in a vote to also deny the club.

This prompted Bridget to file a suit arguing that the Equal Access Act required her school to allow a Christian club alongside other non-curricular clubs since the Act allows the formation of religious, political, philosophical, or other content of the speech groups. The school was subject to the Equal Access Act and the purpose of the Act is to avoid discrimination against a students' religious and political beliefs.

The court held that the school must grant student religious clubs and other student- initiated clubs with the same treatment. The court found that the Equal Access Act does not promote nor endorse religion and

---

[81] 20 U. S. C. A. § 4071(c); Hsu at 857 (footnote 16); Student Coalition for Peace v. Lower Merion School Dist. 776 F. 2d 431 (3rd Cir 1985).

[82] Student Coalition for Peace, 776 F. 2d 431.

[83] (1990) Board of Educ. v. Mergens, 496 U.S. 226

Retrievable at:

https://supreme.justia.com/cases/federal/us/496/226/case.html

therefore does not violate the Establishment Clause, but protects student initiated and student led meetings.

Bridget Mergens won the case, and the court's decision permitted religious activities to take place at Westside High School. This case impacted all of the American public schools by making it crystal clear that Christian clubs are perfectly legal.

CHAPTER 33

WILL SHE HATE ME FOREVER?

My Own Struggle with My Daughter

The sun felt warm on my face as I was relaxing on our deck to enjoy one of the last beautiful fall days. Life was good.

Nina's friend, Melody, came to visit. They were freshmen now. Her mother, Heather, drove her over and decided to come in the house and stay a while to chat. I came in from the deck to talk with her, but Heather wanted me to go back out on the deck with her. I was a little surprised, but soon found out why she wanted to talk in private. In a quivering voice, she said, "Melody doesn't believe in God anymore. She's an atheist now." Heather took a moment to calm herself. "She told me this morning, and I can't believe it. Why would she turn her back on Jesus?"

Looking at Heather, I saw she was crushed. My heart went out to her. I offered to have Nina persuade Melody to go with her to the Christian club at school. Heather thought it was impossible. But Nina tried, and sure enough, Melody did attend a couple of times and even had a better time than expected. Overall, it seemed like it was just too late. Nina told me later that during the worship, Melody's jaw was clamped, during the message, her fists clenched, and the whole while, her heart was closed. She'd been harboring her defiant attitude for too long and had no will to accept faith. Weeks later, Melody explored herself by dressing in men's fashion and cutting her long blonde locks to a pixie cut. Soon after that, she took on a male name.

Little did I know, just a few short months later Nina would give me that same verdict. I also heard those same dreaded words: "Mom I am an atheist now!"

But why? I remember one time when one of her friends came over. They went upstairs in her room. I heard them discuss the Bible and I thought how blessed I was. Instead, I found out that her friend was showing her a passage from the Old Testament that was very difficult to understand at Nina's point in her faith walk, and which caused her to run with fear into the other direction. When Nina told me these points later, I realized that they were talking points from atheistic websites. There were many other instances which she was presented with a reason to doubt and her relationship with God began to fade. Nina's faith started cracking as she was confronted with questions she could not answer.

But we would not find out for months…

Nina started to make more friends in school. They were smart kids from the speech and debate club. When I picked her up after speech competition, I saw all those kids dressed up and courteous, I was pleased. I thought to myself "I am blessed she did not wind up with the wrong crowd, as these kids were eloquent and intelligent."

However, Nina smiled less and argued more. She no longer exhibited her usual joy and typical spring in her step. Nina had become so neutral, not for or against anything, and hidden in her thoughts. I hardly recognized my daughter. Her friends introduced her to their worldly tunes, and she easily strayed from her favorite Christian artists. She played Christian music less and less. Nina used to love her uplifting music, and I thought maybe that's why she was no longer so positive. But I wanted to respect her decisions which included her rights to choose music. I thought she was just exploring new music. I didn't know she was systematically controlled by her so-called friends.

Nina has always been tolerant of other people's lifestyles and accepting of everyone, as we have raised her to be loving and fair. But she had a new boyfriend now, a football player, who attended the Gay-Straight alliance, and he was not so courteous towards other's views.

When Nina said she wanted to attend the Gay-Straight Alliance, I was less than pleased, I finally relented when I saw that she would not take no for an answer. I had no problem with the club itself, and it was okay with me for my daughter to find out their viewpoints because I thought she was strong in her faith.

One day, she came home after the Gay-Straight Alliance club and told me that I know nothing because I believe there are two genders and she was just taught that there are twenty-five gender options. After all, the honors English teacher, her boyfriend's mother, was in charge of that club and told them so. Nina asked me if I knew what this and that type gender was. I had no clue and thus was labeled uneducated and out of date.

Her new friends from the Gay-Straight club were not okay with my daughter's faith although she never expressed anything against their lifestyle. They did not want her to go to the Christian club anymore. In fact, they did not stop putting pressure on her until she gave up her faith. They demanded tolerance and acceptance for their lifestyle but would not extend tolerance nor acceptance for Nina's beliefs nor anyone who believed differently.

Nina was now either enraged or silent whenever we spoke of Christianity. She didn't want to listen to anything about a God whom she felt was unimportant and insignificant. I toned it down and showed respect while praying up a storm, trying to turn her back to God without the familiar Christian reasoning that I'd grown so used to. It became clear that the school and especially her friends were not a good environment and we needed to take her out of it. But she loved her new friends and hung out with at their huge lunch table. It wasn't a question of whether we should take her out of school or not because her behavior turned more and more antagonistic and defiant towards God. Rather the question was: "Will she hate me forever? Will I lose my daughter and get a rebellious teenager? Will she get upset and do even worse?"

I was so upset I started begging God for the answer. I felt led to read the book of Ezra. I said, "Fine, I can do that, but I need an answer here. Please." Then I sensed God saying she would be upset for three days and then she will be fine. I had instant doubt. All I could think of was

Easter and the "three days," and it just seemed like this was not an answer from God, but a Christian cliche I had imagined. My doubt temporarily disconnected me from God. Frustrated, I decided to at least read the book of Ezra.

I almost gave up. Nothing stood out to me in the first five chapters. But then in chapters six to ten there were four occasions where it says: "and after three days". I was stunned. Immediately I knew this was my promise from God. Nina would only be upset for three days. I was so happy and thrilled.

But I still wasn't sure of the best solution for our daughter since we're not cut out for homeschooling. It was two weeks before Christmas, and I wanted Nina to finish the first semester before we pulled her out.

It was a Friday night and Nina was getting ready for a party with the speech and debate team. I saw a message pop up on her computer which was very explicit and disturbing information from her boyfriend. I knew she needed to leave the school right away. I was afraid and shaking as I marched up to her bathroom where she put on the final makeup touches, all ready for the party. With all the courage I could muster, I said: "Nina you're not going to the party. You're also not going to the speech debate tomorrow. Nor will you ever go back to that school."

Nina was devastated. We had a teenage terror that night as she barricaded herself in her room. She was heartbroken, but after a while, she let me talk to her, but too hurt to respond much. Finally, she fell asleep. I was afraid she'd escape through her second-floor bedroom window although it was nearly impossible.

God woke me up in the middle of the night and said, "go pray for Nina". So, I got up and sat by her bedside laying my hand on her leg and just prayed up a storm. She never woke up and I went back to sleep.

The next morning, I went into Nina's room not knowing what to expect. I sat on the sofa across her bed and she opened her eyes. Then she said, "I get why you don't want me to go back, and I think that you have a point. But it doesn't seem like I have much choice in the matter, so I might as well try to find the good in it. I'll break up with my boyfriend.

He's not a good influence. And I don't like my high school anyhow. I already did some college courses at Malone University. Maybe I can do more of that."

I couldn't believe my ears. I was so happy. It had only been one day, not even three days.

And sure enough. She broke up with her boyfriend. I admit that I was glad. After all, he put a wedge between me and my daughter.

But he didn't give up so easily. He was excruciatingly sweet to Nina afterward. He even got his and her friends to tell her how great a person he was. It was the second day they were getting close again. Nina got upset when I said something about him.

That Sunday night, we had teenage terror again. I was worried and scared, so I asked my husband to stay home from work on Monday. He reminded me he had no vacation days left. I insisted and told him I didn't want to be alone when she woke up.

Once again, the Lord woke me up in the middle of the night and had me pray for her. I prayed fervently. She lifted her head in the middle of the prayer and looked straight at me. The light was off, so I could only see the silhouette of her head. I couldn't see if her eyes were open. She put her head down again, and I kept praying up the storm. One more time she lifted her head. It was almost scary. So, I said Amen and Good Night and left in a hurry. I was glad my husband stayed home, but we should have known he could have at least worked half a day as our teenager didn't wake up until 1 p.m.!

Again, I was on the couch in her room waiting for my daughter to wake up. Just like last time when she woke up she looked at me and said: "I made the right decision to break up with him. And I do want to do College Credit Plus."

It was the third day and what God made clear to me came to pass. Nina wasn't mad at me. She didn't want her school nor boyfriend back.

Sure enough, Nina stayed firm and enrolled in college full-time. She didn't even have to take one high school course that Spring semester as she aligned her college courses so they would count for high school. She's now a sophomore in High School and a sophomore in college.

However, Nina still didn't believe in God and requested I respect that. We told her she didn't have to go to church and we would not talk to her as if she were a Christian. But we said because she listened to all those atheists, it was only fair to listen to Christian evidence such as archeology to get the whole picture. She agreed, and as a family, we studied the book: "A Case for Christ" by Lee Strobel every day. About two weeks into the book, in the fourth chapter her faith was restored. Now she's very active with the youth group in church.

I attend a Bible group in our city where some of moms have teenagers in public schools. They informed me that the Gay-Straight Alliance was very popular at their schools as well. Other mothers told me how in their schools, secularism and even Satanism is rampant. It was just another confirmation about the environments that bombard our children every single day.

We often hope that our children can be the salt and the light. Often those who select their friends carefully and don't let themselves be negatively influenced are the bright lights in schools. Others who have a high need for connectivity and friendships might sacrifice their faith if they don't find Christian friends. Linking Christians together provides a fortress that makes falling away more difficult.

Maybe our daughter's case was extreme. She was an outstanding Christian before and even broke up with a Christian boyfriend in middle school because he wasn't godly enough. Nina told me of numerous Christian friends who had lost their faith. Looking at statistics, many Christian kids tend to fall away from their belief in God while attending public schools.

Barna research shows that those kids never come back to God even in adulthood. They also released a recent study stating that ninety-eight percent of Christians are not sharing their faith with non-Christians. Comparing that to the strong lobby of atheism and their full-on prosetilyzing efforts in our public schools we need to support our Christian kids that much more.

Nina needed support to find her way back to God. I believe that if she had been more strongly involved in the Christian club with Godly friends, she would have fared much better than hanging out with atheists. I realize that the Christian club is just one of the components. Church and home are just as important. We are now glad we pulled her out of that environment, and she's a strong Christian again, doing all her high school work in college via the college credit plus program. What the devil means for evil God turns around for good.

Christian clubs are so important because students can freely express their opinions without being judged or belittled. It's a place to find friends and support and is a refuge in stormy waters. With anti-God clubs on the rise, it's of paramount importance for Christian students to band together.

"See, I am doing a new thing! Now it springs up; do you not perceive it? I am making a way in the wilderness and streams in the wasteland."
Isaiah 43:19

CHAPTER 34

GAY-STRAIGHT CLUBS AND THE LGBT COMMUNITY

A dialogue between two students who are neither attending the Christian nor the LGBT clubs....

"Oh no. Here she comes with her tracts."

"Quick, let's dash and get a desert," said Julia.

"Ha, ha! It worked. I'm so sick and tired of this. Why does she feel she has to convert me? Am I not good enough?" asked Kayla.

"Let it go. Everyone knows you're helping with Big Brother Big Sister and are always helping people. You have better morals than most people, including some Christians".

"But they should know that, too. This school is not that big. We know each other. There's got to be another reason," said Kayla.

"I guess it's the same with the Gay-Straight Alliance Club. Why does the GSA club constantly invite people. They are relentless in trying to sign up people for their club," said Julia.

"They must just believe in telling everybody about the GSA club and that we're not born with a set biological sex. They just want their belief to be accepted in society and for people to be tolerant and inclusive of their views. I get that."

"Well then, why not let the Christians do the same thing? Why be offended at what they do and be intolerant of Christian clubs?" Julia asked.

"I guess. Maybe they should all quit," muttered Kayla.

"That's freedom of speech. We all have the right to standup for what we believe", said Julia.

"Fine let's just enjoy our dessert."

But Why?

A book on Christian clubs would not be complete without addressing current trends in our public schools affecting Christianity. It takes a paradigm shift to reach this new generation. We cannot wish reality away. Instead, we need to face it and be the light in the midst of it. And that light will illuminate new and wonderful opportunities.

Shocking Statistics

The US Department of Health and Human Services/Centers for Disease Control and Prevention MMWR / August 12, 2016, report states:

The following students seriously considered attempting suicide during the 12 months before the survey.

> 17.7% of all high school students;
> 14.8% of heterosexual students;
> 42.8% of gay, lesbian, or bisexual students; and
> 31.9% of students who are not sure of their sexual identity

The prevalence of having seriously considered attempting suicide was higher among gay, lesbian, and bisexual students (42.8%) than heterosexual students (14.8%)[84]

These percentages are sky high for all students, but especially for the

---

[84] US Department of Health and Human Services/Centers for Disease Control and Prevention MMWR / August 12, 2016 / Vol. 65 / No. 9 19

LGBT students. It's crucial to communicate in a manner which is uplifting and loving.

How can we love people who have a different lifestyle without sacrificing our convictions? Can we accept another lifestyle without approving it? Are you on the side of love or the side of truth? Is it more important to show the love of God or to show the truth of the scriptures?

Is it our responsibility to point out the wrong in certain lifestyles? No doubt, at some point, there is a person and place for direct talk as long as it's in a loving setting. But, does that burden have to be on high schoolers so they will be labeled homophobes? Can we accept people as individuals made in the image of God even if we don't approve of their life choice? Why is this so important?

Who Can Cast a Stone?

As an example of a different lifestyle, let's look at the story of the adulterous woman and how Jesus responded in John 8:3-7:

"The Scribes and the Pharisees brought a woman who had been caught in adultery, and placing her in the midst, they said to him, "Teacher, this woman has been caught in the act of adultery. Now, in the Law, Moses commanded us to stone such women. So what do you say? This they said to test him, that they might have some charge to bring against him. Jesus bent down and wrote with his finger on the ground." And as they continued to ask him, he stood up and said to them, "Let him who is without sin among you be the first to throw a stone at her."

This is a tremendous statement about being judgmental toward the adulterous woman and ultimately all sinners. Jesus said that only the sinless were worthy of casting the first stone.

Christians should neither condone sin nor be judgmental of it. Judgment is God's role, not ours. We are to pray, offer guidance, and show compassion. While not easy, this stance shows a glimpse of true Christian love. The scriptures say, "by your love shall they know."

Verses 8-9 state: "And once more he bent down and wrote on the ground. But when they heard it, they went away one by one, beginning with the older ones, and Jesus was left alone with the woman standing before him."

Jesus showed respect and mercy. He did not condemn the adulterous woman. After He mentioned, "whoever is without sin should throw the first stone," he sat down again and wrote on the ground. He merely stated that whoever is without sin can point the finger at the woman who had a different life choice.

It's interesting that Jesus also showed respect for people who were harsh with the woman. Instead of ordering them to leave he gave them space by sitting on the ground again writing. Jesus values free choice and free will for all. He did not condemn or stare down the accusers so they would leave. He never ordered them to leave. He wanted people to make their own decision by putting the mirror before their face. Then, one by one, and of their own volition, they all left.

Verses 10-11 state: Jesus stood up and said to her, "Woman, where are they? Has no one condemned you?" She said, "No one, Lord." And Jesus said, "Neither do I condemn you; go, and from now on sin no more."

Even though Jesus acknowledged the fact that he did not agree with her life style, Jesus did not condemn her. Instead, He offered forgiveness.

Do We Need to Clean Up Our Lives Before God Accepts Us?

Does God expect people to be perfect when they approach him? Does God sit on a huge throne high above being unreachable to us?

Jesus told the parable about leaving the ninety-nine sheep to find that one lost sheep. Jesus was delighted when the lost one came back. And the father of the prodigal son threw him a party when he came back even though the son squandered away his inheritance. That's how the scriptures define God and offer a prime example of good Christian conduct.

Are we the ones who are responsible for convicting people of their sin when the Holy Spirit can cut between bone and marrow and read people's mail? The Holy Spirit won't come across as judging or critical but as the Bible calls him "our Comforter." Is that reserved for those who already believe in God or is the Holy Spirit willing to reach out and touch any soul? How many stories have we heard of God through the Holy Spirit embracing people with an almost palpable love surrounding them? "No one comes to God except the Holy Spirit draws them."[85] Can we show people our love and acceptance before demanding a perfect life style? Could they find God by this?

How Can Two Percent of the Population Cause Such a Stir?

I've found that many LGBTQ people think Christians consider them the worst of sinners and that there's no spot for them in heaven. Naturally, this belief makes that life-style community defensive. Defensiveness coupled with Christian judgement builds a wall between the two. The resulting fear of rejection keeps that community away from Christians. Even the expectation of rejection and the mere anticipation of it ruffles up feathers. Fear, anxiety, isolation, substance abuse and suicide are challenges in that community according to Brian Rood, Ph.D., MPH, assistant professor of psychology at Augsburg College. [86]That's why they put up such a fight for their rights. This is perfectly understandable as we all want to stand up for our rights, however, in recent years some of that fight is resulting in being less and sometimes even intolerant toward Christians.

Has the Underdog Become the Aggressor?

Does the LGBT community enjoy more rights than Christians do now? Are politicians catering more to that community because of strong lobbying and advocacy? I have often wondered how the LGBT community can demand people to be inclusive and tolerant while many won't offer that themselves to the Christian community.

Fear of rejection may be the reason for that. But the tide is turning. The LGBT community has strengthened to the point where it's hard to tell who is the victim and who is the bully. It has come to canceling and censoring other's opinions and demanding to have your way regardless of other's rights such as Christian rights.

---

[85] For no one can come to me unless the Father who sent me draws them to me, and at the last day I will raise them up. John 6:44 New Living Translation

[86] Garofalo, R. (2018). Transgender Health . Retrievable at: http://www.liebertpub.com/overview/transgender-health/634/

Despite all of that, especially as Christians we should strive to reach out in love. We need to choose about where we stand on the spectrum between grace and truth. Is it more important for us to show God's grace and love or biblical truth. What needs to be our starting point? Are we obligated to point out the truth from the start or can we offer friendship and acceptance so people can discover truth along their path? And are we willing to be close enough on that path should questions arise?

Getting Support

We need to be strong in our faith when opening up to people who tend to distrust and disdain God or who even outright ridicule faith. Your Christian support network is critical to withstanding attacks on your faith. As seen elsewhere in this book, my daughter, who was a strong Christian in high school, was proselytized by the Gay-Straight club, which was predominantly atheistic. In essence, they stole her faith and made an atheist out of my daughter. Somehow, they could not accept her as a Christian.

But soon she realized that it also takes faith to accept life without the explanation of a higher power, and she found the Christian faith to be more plausible. However, this turnaround would not have happened without Christian support. High school is difficult even without the faith component. Everyone is struggling to fit in. High schoolers don't have much life experience to make decisions and are overly self conscious. That's why it's important for Christians to find a group to connect and belong.

How Can We Reach People of That Community

Why not invite people with a different lifestyle into your community? Sadly, most won't come, but you can still maintain some form of friendship to be available when needed.

When people see we put love before our theological conviction they might realize that the real God is different than what they expected. Why not err on the side of mercy? Matt: 5:7 states, "Blessed are the merciful, for they [themselves] will be shown mercy." And verse 9 says, "Blessed are the peacemakers, for they will be called children of God."

Here are some suggestions for conversations with the LGBT community.

- o Get to know people for who they are intellectually rather than sexually
- o Connect rather than reject
- o Refrain from preaching; chances are they've heard it all before
- o Talk about their journey with God and share yours
- o Love wins out over any debate or argument, always

As stated earlier it might be best to let God draw them instead of us pushing people before they are ready. Our lifestyle and our love are the greatest witness to this community.

When we reach others who are open and interested, our silent witness in love may draw others in we couldn't reach if we had tried.

Gay-Straight Cubs

Gay-Straight Clubs have changed the landscape of our high schools with gender identity teaching. GSA clubs were established in 1998 and today the vast majority of our high schools have such a club. The purpose of this book is not to get into the full debate of it. Rather we need to work with this well-established community which is not retreating. Those clubs do provide a service to the school by helping protect the LGBT community. The problem is that they also promote that kind of lifestyle to impressionable and vulnerable teenagers. Nonetheless, it's critical to extend Christian love.

Gay-Straight Alliance Network has changed its name to Genders & Sexualities Alliance Network in 2016. The national LGBTQ youth organization also unveiled a new tagline: "trans and queer youth uniting for racial and gender justice."[87]

Now that Gay-Straight Clubs have included racial justice they will recruit the African American community for growth and strength and to further their agenda.

---

[87] Carter, B. (2016). GSA Network Unveils New Name and Tagline.
Retrievable at:
https://gsanetwork.org/GSA-Network-Unveils-New-Name-and-Tagline

I wish Christians would advocate just as much for their own beliefs. Gay-Straight Alliance Network directors say in a statement: "GSA clubs have been a powerful force for societal change[88].."

Are Christians More Moral than Others?

We also need to steer clear of thinking that Christians hold the monopoly on moral behavior. Such prejudice is offensive and divisive and therefore serves no purpose. Some Christians believe that all morals ultimately stem from the Bible. That might well be, but morals can still be upheld without believing in God. No doubt you all know relatives, friends, or coworkers who are better people than some Christians. Even though Bible stories are helpful in teaching morals, they don't have the exclusive right.

Even though many members of the Gay-Straight Alliance do not believe in God, some do hold portions of worthwhile morals, and it's important to acknowledge this as well. Focusing on where we intersect rather than where we differ can be important in bringing peace and change.

Awareness and Respect

We just need to be aware of the GSA clubs and know their objectives and concerns about faith. This way we won't step on their toes. Then we will be knowledgeable enough to come into dialogue. As long as there is mutual respect on both sides, problems can be averted.

Focus on building the Christian Club

Ultimately, we need to focus on our objectives and stand up for our rights by establishing or growing Christian clubs. We don't need to start out by trying to proof to atheists that God exists. Of course, we always need to be ready should someone ask. Our initial objective should be to focus on gathering Christians who share beliefs rather than opposing other viewpoints.

High school students often just join the popular club, whichever one it is. Therefore we need to put in at least as much effort as the GSA

[88] ibid

promoters do with their campaigns. In fact, let's triple that effort!

The following is an interesting article about this subject from the Family Research Council:

April 21, 2017

Florida School Up to Its Necklace in Trouble[89]

"Making a fashion statement wasn't the point of a ninth grader's cross necklace in Florida. Making a statement of faith was. And to her LGBT activist teacher, that was the problem. At Riverview High School in Hillsborough, a freshman girl barely set down her books on her desk when Ms. Lora Riedas pointed to her small cross pendant and said, "I need you to take your necklace off." Stunned, the girl asked why. The teacher refused to answer and instead barked that it was "disrespectful" and repeated her demand. Not wanting to seem disrespectful, the teenager did what she was told.

Upset, her parents contacted our friends at Liberty Counsel who sent a letter to the superintendent explaining[90] that it was the teacher who was disrespectful. "In banning cross necklaces from three different students in her classroom, Ms. Riedas has "intentionally violate[d] or den[ied] a student's legal rights." The right to wear a cross necklace is clearly established. There is no question that students have the right to wear religious jewelry, despite any specious claim of 'gang affiliation' by Ms. Riedas. Subsequent to her cross ban, Ms. Reidas has subjected at least one of the students 'to unnecessary embarrassment or disparagement,' in singling the student out for false allegations of student behavior violations"…

…At the beginning of the year, Liberty Counsel[91] points out, she put

---

[89] Perkins, T. (2017). Florida School up to Its Necklace in Legal Trouble .
Retrievable at:
http://www.frc.org/updatearticle/20170421/florida-school
[90] Eakins, J. (2017). Legal Correspondence.
[91] Smith, S. (2017). Florida Teacher Bans Cross Necklaces in Class, Promotes LGBT Day of Silence .
Retrievable at:

rainbow stickers on her students' folders without their permission. When one student peeled hers off, she noticed that she was treated with more hostility than her peers. Talk about hypocrisy! This teacher is banning crosses on one hand and engaging in "wholesale LGBT activism" on the other. If anything's offensive, it's that! "Ms. Riedas has further engaged in impermissible LGBT political activism in the classroom, and has indicated her intent to further do so during instructional time," the letter claims. "Ms. Riedas is planning to promote GLSEN's 'Day of Silence' coercive political activities during instructional time in her classroom this April 21, 2017."

None of this is a surprise to Ms. Riedas's Twitter followers. The teacher's feed is full of advice about "how to talk to kids about what it means to be an LGBT ally" and how to engage on the transgender bathroom issue. And according to school policy, posting these things isn't the problem -- posting them during class hours is.

As Liberty Counsel reminds Riverview High, "It is the policy of the Board that students, staff members, and District facilities not be used for promoting the interests of any non-school agency or organization, public or private, without the approval of the superintendent."

Together with her attorneys, this brave ninth grader is asking for the right to express her faith, which is already guaranteed to her by the Constitution. Students should never have to check their beliefs at the school house door -- or anywhere else for that matter.

---

http://www.christianpost.com/news/florida-teacher-bans-cross-necklaces-in-class-promotes-lgbt-day-of-silence-181167/

CHAPTER 35

HOW TO SET UP A HIGH SCHOOL CHRISTIAN CLUB

High School Clubs can be set up using one of these two laws:

1. Equal Access Act
2. First Amendment Free Speech Clause

Advantages Of Setting It Up Via The Equal Access Act

Principals and school administration are more familiar with the Equal Access Act because most of the clubs are set up this way and are run as student-led clubs. Principals might automatically give you the paperwork to fill out for an Equal Access Club.

Disadvantages of the Equal Access Act

Even though the Equal Access Act provides equal access for all types of clubs, the Christian club is more limited than other clubs when it comes to leadership. Other clubs can have more adult involvement. For example, a teacher can teach the chess club or a volunteer can teach the drama club. But a volunteer such as a community leader, youth pastor or parent cannot lead the Christian club. It has to be student led. However as mentioned elsewhere in the book, students can invite outside speakers as long as that speaker does not speak more often than every four times of club meetings. But students can invite different speakers every week if they wish.

The Equal Access Act does not mandate teacher sponsors. Therefore sponsors are determined by individual school policies. That's why it's important to obtain a copy of your school policy on clubs to learn your school's rules about sponsorships.

If the school does require club sponsors, it's important to know that although teacher sponsors of other clubs are allowed to participate and teach in their club, the act stipulates that the sponsors of Christian clubs can only attend in a non-participatory function. This is to prevent the appearance that the school is trying to establish religion thus violating the establishment clause. For Christian clubs, the teacher sponsor will only be there to monitor the club for safety purposes.

Advantages Of A Christian Club Set Up Via The First Amendment Free Speech Clause

The great advantage of setting up a club this way is that the club does not have to be student run. In fact, it can be entirely run by your youth pastor. And the youth pastor can teach every single week. Youth pastors know how to build and grow youth groups or Christian clubs. The youth pastor will still need your help in connecting with other students and inviting them to come, but he or she will know how to create an atmosphere and make it inviting and fun.

So if you have a principal who is more open towards a Christian club you might want to take this route because it's easier on you and the club has a better chance to succeed since an experienced person is starting and running it.

However, you might have to educate your principal on that type of a club because they are so used to setting up a club via the Equal Access Act.

Disadvantages Of A Christian Club Set Up By The First Amendment Free Speech Clause.

Since many principals are not that familiar with this kind of community club, it's more difficult to set up. It would be best for you to find out where your principal stands. But bear in mind, even if the principal is open and fair towards Christians it does not mean that he or she is willing to do something they are not familiar with, even if it is legal. Many principals fear the relentless push of atheists and take the easy route.

So Which One Is Best?

It depends on two factors:

1. Your Christian club leadership team and
2. The openness of your principal.

If it's a reserved and shy team, you might be better off by having a youth pastor run it via the First Amendment. Same with if you have a youth pastor who's on fire and wants to reach out to the school. He or she can be involved from the very first meeting with the principal and even come along to the meeting.

However, a determined student leader who is willing to reach out to other Christians would be better off with a student led Equal Access Club because it's easier to set up and won't be challenged as much by administration nor atheists. Plus that student along with the whole club leadership team can still be fully mentored by the youth pastor. The pastor can provide lessons and help with planning just like any mentor or coach.

But if the principal is Christian and open to your club, it would still be advisable to start a Free Speech Club.

The following chapter describes a Christian Club set up via the Equal Access Act.....

CHAPTER 36

EQUAL ACCESS ACT CLUB STORY

Fictional Explanation

"Now that Mr. Graham finally agreed to meet with us, we need to decide what kind of club we want," said Chloe.

Amelia thought for a moment and then remembered that they could start a club using either the Free Speech Rights or the Equal Access Act.

"We need to make up our mind which way to go. It was already difficult to schedule a meeting with the principal. Going with the Equal Access Act may be the better option because he's familiar with it. All the other school clubs are using the Equal Access Act."

"That's true," said Chloe, but then we have to do all the teaching ourselves because the Equal Access Act stipulates that adults, like our youth pastor, cannot run it. So, it has to be student-led. If we'd go with the First Amendment's Free Speech Rights, we could have an adult teach it. We wouldn't have to do it all ourselves."

"I thought you told me a while ago that even with an Equal Access Club we can invite people like Pastor Sam for about every fourth meeting. And we could invite other speakers and rotate them the same way. And, there are videos and lessons online. You know that Rob likes videos. We can ask where he finds his," said Amelia." And I bet Pastor Sam would help, plus he can still be our mentor. He just can't be at the meetings all the time, right? So, he's allowed to walk us through this as long as he's not the one who teaches the club at school. That's something we have to do ourselves. But we can meet with him every week to get it going."

"Yes, he could mentor us and show us what do. I know he's even allowed to help us plan the lessons so we can teach them," said Chloe. "Okay I'll try and arrange that meeting with Pastor Sam."

After church, the two teens hung around to speak with Pastor Sam. It took quite a while before he was finally alone.

Hey, Pastor Sam, we have a meeting scheduled with our principal to ask about starting a Christian club, but the only way to do it is if we teach it ourselves. The problem is that we're not exactly the most experienced teachers," said Chloe.

"That's amazing! I'm happy that you girls have such passion. I'd be glad to help you, but we'll have to be careful about it. I'm not sure if the law allows it, with the Separation of Church and State and all," said Pastor Sam with a little hesitation.

"No worries, we got that covered. Separation of Church and State just means that you can't push religion on everyone -- like you can't preach about God in school assemblies. But you can have clubs anytime as long as they are voluntary. This way it doesn't violate the Establishment Clause. The clubs are protected by the First Amendment Free Speech Clause," said Amelia.

"So, we can have a club at our school, too?" questioned Ashley, who happened to be nearby.

"Sure," said Amelia. "I can text you more about it later."

"Thanks! Maybe I can talk with you guys more about it? I'd like to hear from you, too, Pastor Sam," said Ashley.

"Sounds good," said Amelia.

"Can I come, too?" said Ashley's friend Megan.

"How about it Pastor? Can we have a meeting together sometime?

Maybe after-school at around 4:30 here at the church Wednesday?' said Chloe.

"I like that idea," said Pastor Sam.

"That should work for me too," said Megan.

As Chloe and Amelia walk up to the church that Wednesday they run into Megan and Ashley in the parking lot. Megan is so excited that she brought them donuts.

Pastor Sam had just arrived. "Hi, young ladies. Good to see you again. Oh, and you brought donuts. It's getting serious now. That's my philosophy for youth group. Have some fun and food, and people will come. You can never go wrong with donuts or pizza."

As they settled into the comfy chairs in the youth group room, Pastor Sam looked at the four youth group members filled with the sense of joy and pride. "They're doing it," he marveled. "They're living out what I've been teaching them." He sure needed something positive like this after his crazy week the'd had trying to help teenagers in difficult situations.

"Okay, how in the world can we start a Christian club at school?" said Chloe. "Even though the principal approved it, it's kind of scary now to get started. What if no one comes? What if it's a flop. That would be so embarrassing."

"Why don't you play it safe then?" Pastor Sam retorted.

What do you mean, Pastor Sam?

"Do you know other Christians in the school?" he replied.

"Yeah, some, but not too many," said Amelia.

"That's okay. You can try and get that handful of people together, like in kind of a dream team, for a Christian club. First, speak to them individually after class or over lunch. Find out if they would like to get together with other Christians like once every week or every other week. Remind them that it's good to encourage each other and be there for each other and just have fun together as Christians."

"Sure, we can do that," said Chloe, with the others nodding.

After you have spoken to five or ten people, you can all meet together like a dream team and discuss it. At that meeting, you can ask each one to identify another two to three Christians that they know and encourage them to talk to those students before next week's planning meeting.

"That's a great idea because everyone knows someone. And this way we can get the word out," said Amelia.

"Exactly. Once you have ten to twenty people, you've got your club. Then you can come up with a cool name for your club and some guidelines for how to structure the club if you want," said Pastor Sam.

"Yeah, but what about the teaching?" wondered Chloe again.

"Yeah, that's the next step. You need to make it interesting, fun and inviting, so people want to come. Let's go over some fun lessons next time we meet. Also, please bring along a list of people you've invited."

Chloe and Amelia were so glad that Megan and Ashley had the same lunch period. From that day on they huddled together at lunch, strategizing, hoping, fretting, but mostly being so excited about their new venture.

"Okay, I got two people I can ask," blurted Chloe.

I also got two," mentioned Megan.

"Alright, with my three," said Amelia, "we can talk to seven people this week. Let's be sure to pray for each other and that those people will be open."

About a week later, the girls had already talked to their intended friends. While meeting with Pastor Sam, they gave their news.

"Hey, both of mine said they're interested," said Megan.

Chloe also said: "One of mine said she has swimming after school every day. But the other one can come."

"Mine want to know more about it. Actually, why don't we invite all the people we spoke to so far to the dream-team meeting with Pastor Sam next week?"

"Good idea," said Chloe.

"Hey" said Pastor Sam, "if this keeps up pretty soon you need two boxes of donuts."

"Yeah, so far so good," the girls uttered, pretty proud of themselves.

"Got a nice group together already. That's the way to do it. Keep finding people by talking to as many Christians as you know. Then, once you have a good group together, you can be a little more vocal by passing out flyers and having it announced on the intercom. And you could plan some fun activities to attract non-Christians."

"That sounds good. Now, what about the lesson?"

"Sure. Do you want to have a guest speaker or a video?" said Pastor Sam, "or do you want your club to be more interactive?"

The girls looked at each other, clueless.

"I guess interaction is good so we get to know each other better and connect better right?" Megan said.

"I agree, we don't want to have another long lesson the end of the day", offered Amelia.

"Do you know of some like short videos that would cover some interesting themes for Christians in high schools and serve as a discussion starter?" Amelia queried.

"Sure, there are lots of such videos, and some even come with discussion questions. And lots of youth group lessons are available. I can bring you some materials next week," said Pastor Sam.

"That would be great," said Chloe.

"So, we could either use video clips, a book or even a speaker. That's cool. We better have some official leaders in the club who can make those decisions so there won't be a power struggle," said Amelia.

"Good point. Also, have you thought of a name for the club?" asked Pastor Sam.

"Why not just call it the Christian club," said Megan.

"I don't know. How about a catchier name?" said Amelia.

"Well you come up with one," Chloe muttered.

"How about *The Tribe*, *The Fish*, or *The Huddle*. I don't know, it's kind of important to have a good name, and we can take our time," said Amelia.

"You know, none of those names are bad," Chloe interjected.

"I'm not sure. Why don't we sit on it for a week and think it through," said Amelia.

"Okay what's next on the list," said Chloe.

"Hey, do we have a list?" joked the new kid.

Pastor Sam chimed in and said: "What about music? Do you want to have music before and after the meeting for the atmosphere?"

"Yeah, why not, I think that would create a good atmosphere," said Chloe. "Who can handle the music?"

Megan said: "I can just play my play list on my smartphone and bring a portable speaker. Or if we have a classroom with a Smart Board, I can go on the Internet and play a YouTube video."

"The video would be great, but if we don't have that capability the phone will work too," said Amelia.

"Okay ,music is checked off. What else?" said Chloe.

"Don't forget about the food," said Pastor Sam.

"How about we just make a schedule, and each one of us takes care of one week. Maybe we could ask our moms to help out."

"That's a good idea," said Amelia. "Do you want to be in charge of that, Travis?"

Travis nodded. He was thrilled to be a part of this new venture.

"How about we do something fun, too," Zack, another new kid piped in. "I agree, for starters, we could use some icebreakers," said Chloe. "Plus, games on top of that. Are you game for it, Zack?"

"Sure, I'd love too. Here's a good one I heard of: You bring a roll of toilet paper. Then you pass it around. Each one has to take one or more sheets. They can take as many sheets as they want. When the roll has passed around and comes back to you, you say: Now tell us one personal thing about yourself for each sheet you took." Zack offered excitedly. "Just google *icebreakers for youth groups*."

"Cool, it looks like Amelia and I will look into speakers, and Travis will handle the food. Megan will be in charge of the music and and Zack of the icebreakers and games. Wow, we sure covered enough for today," said Chloe.

Everyone seemed quite impressed with their new dream team.

"Can each of us find another two to three Christian students and bring them to the dream team next time? Then we can discuss more about the lessons. Same time same day next week?" said Amelia.

"Pastor Sam, I know we kind of took over the meeting but you'll come next week again, right?" said Chloe

"Of course, I'll bring some lesson ideas too. Really, the more you catch on the better. This group has great ideas and is willing to act on them. Good for you. Let's keep this drenched in prayer too. See you guys next week."

CHAPTER 37

FIRST AMENDMENT CLUB STORY

Fictional Explanation

"I know it's easier to set up a Christian club using the Equal Access Rights, but I want to use the First Amendment Right. This way we can have Pastor Jeff run it, and that would be so cool," said Chloe.

"You think he'd even do it?" said Amelia.

"Well, let's talk to him after church or youth group."

Pastor Jeff got on board. "Wow, that was easy, so glad he's excited about this. I will set up a meeting with the principal," said Amelia.

Amelia, Chloe and Pastor Jeff snagged a meeting with the principal. He wasn't as enthusiastic. "I can't have an adult run a student club," the principal stated with a firm voice.

"I see adults teach the gay-straight club all the time," said Chloe.

"That's different. Only Christian clubs have that restriction with the Equal Access Act because only a Christian or Atheistic club can violate the Establishment Clause, " said the principal. Chloe knew that was true.

"We don't want an Equal Access Club. We want to set up our club using the First Amendment Rights, so that adults can teach it. As you know, there was a case about this which went all the way up to the Supreme

Court. And the Supreme Court decided in favor of the Christian Club and against the School. Here is a copy of the Milford case to refresh your memory," said Amelia, "I could never do as good a job as Pastor Jeff can, so when I found out that according to the Milford case he's legally allowed to teach the club, I asked him to consider," said Chloe " and it turns out he would love to help."

"Yes," said Pastor Jeff, "I've read from all these documents here, that the Department of Education wants the community to get involved with our schools. Even the faith-based community. That's what I'm here for."

"Sure, that's true. But you can help from the sidelines. You don't need to teach. In high school, students need to learn to lead, so this would be a prime opportunity for you girls to step out of your comfort zone," insisted the principal. "I'll approve the club as an Equal Access Club right now. That's how every other club is set up. Trust me, in this school, this is the only way to start a club."

"We appreciate that," said Chloe, "and hope you know that we thought this through. We want a Free Speech Club, and these documents will show you that we have that right. Please look at this highlighted paragraph in the Milford case I just gave you. That's the Supreme Court decision allowing Christian Clubs based on our First Amendment Free Speech rights. Our rights are crystal clear. And here is a list of organizations supporting Christian Clubs. Do you see the Department of Education, The White House and even the ACLU supporting our rights? I think you will appreciate the following reports," Chloe added, handing him several documents.

- Student Rights
- Guidance on Religious Expression in Public Schools
- Public schools and religious Communities
- Religion in the Public Schools: A Joint Statement Of Current Law (highlight Nr 13)
- List of Organizations with more Information

"I've highlighted the parts which apply to our situation."

And if we ever have a flyer, we can put a statement on there saying that this is not a school-sponsored event. Here is a sample handout for that.

See what it says:"

The United States Constitution requires schools to respect the right of all external organizations to distribute flyers to students at school if the school permits any such organization to distribute flyers. Accordingly, the school cannot discriminate among groups wishing to distribute flyers at school and does not endorse the content of any flyer distributed at school. The school encourages parents to assist their students in making choices appropriate for them. This is not an activity of the school or the School District.

The principal began looking over those documents with an intense expression. Seeing he could not change their minds and that the law was on their side, he said: "Looks like you've done your homework," he admitted grudgingly, "Now, our school district approves community organizations on a district level. I can't even make that decision here for this school, only once it's approved, I get to decide if it's good for my school. But the Equal Access Clubs are approved automatically for all schools while this has to be approved separately by the school district."

"We understand," Chloe added. "In fact, we already did a presentation to the roundtable of principals. I guess you missed that meeting. But our high school club program was approved for all schools in the district. Mrs. Malone at the city school board is our coordinator. You can talk to her, but here is the letter stating that we're approved," she said, handing the principal the letter.

"Well, alright then. It looks like you did your homework. In that case, Congratulations to your new Christian Club. Do you have a name for it yet?" the principal queried.

Please note that this is a scenario with a principal who tries to prevent the club. Most principals will not be that averse to a Christian club. And, most school districts don't require a roundtable presentation. But principals will still not be very familiar with the Free Speech club setup. So, you will have to be fully prepared for that meeting. It's always good to be prepared for a worst-case scenario like this one.

CHAPTER 38

INSTRUCTIONS TO SET UP A CLUB

Equal Access Club Instructions

This club has to be set up by students, not adults, because it's student-led.

Look for other people who want to build or grow a Christian club.

1. Find another student to help set up the Christian Club together.
2. Research the school to find out if another club is already in existence.

   A) If yes: Join the club and pour all your energies into helping that club grow. Don't just start a competitive club unless there are solid reasons to do so.

   B) If no: Talk to stakeholders such as other Christian students and Christian teachers/secretaries/staff for feedback. Involve people early on so they take ownership. This will motivate them to invest energies into building the club. If you make all the decisions first and call it your club, people will not be as motivated to help you grow the club.

3. Get together with your friend and write out a list of names of students and teachers who are open to a Christian club.

4. Tackle that list and decide which one of you is going to talk to which Christian teacher. Speak to at least two or more teachers/staff to find out the following:

A) Where the principal stands regarding a Christian club.
B) If the school requires teacher sponsors for club meetings.
C) If they would let you use their classroom for the club meetings.

5. Decide which teacher you want to ask to be a teacher sponsor if required by the school. Even if it's not required, you can approach that teacher for help.

6. Communicate your plan to your parents and youth group and ask for prayer. No need to do this all on your own. God wants to be on your side.

7. Talk to your friends in church youth group and find out what other schools are doing. See if you can attend one of their meetings or talk to their student leader.

8. Disclose your interest to your youth pastor and ask to meet with him/her. They might well know other youth pastors or students who are involved in such a club.

The following instructions are for adults such as youth pastors, parents or community organization leaders:

First Amendment Club Instructions

This Type of club can be set up by either students or by youth pastors, parents, or community organization leaders.

Adult Setup

As a youth pastor or any concerned adult who wants to leave a positive impact on the schools you still need to find out the same information as mentioned earlier such as:

- ✓ Find out if the school already has a Christian club.
- ✓ Meet the club leaders and offer your help.
- ✓ If your school has no Christian club yet, talk to stakeholders such as other Christian students and Christian teachers/

secretaries/staff for feedback. Involve people early on, so they take ownership. This will motivate them to invest energies into building the club. If you make all the decisions first and call it your club people will not be as motivated to help grow the club.

✓ Research both the school district website and the local school website for club policies. You sometimes find them lumped in with the entire school board policies.

✓ Find out if the principal is open to a Christian club and if the school requires teacher sponsors for club meetings.

✓ Identify students from your church who attend that school and involve them in a strategy meeting.

✓ Follow your school board directions on community clubs and submit your plans.

✓ Find a student who is interested in helping to establish the club. That student can make an appointment with the principal for you, and you can attend together. It would be incredibly hard for you to obtain a meeting with the principal alone. Trust me; we've tried many times. Therefore, I would not even try to do that because if the principal or secretary turns you down, it's difficult to attend another meeting with the student. Therefore, be sure to let the student set up that meeting and attend together.

Student Set-Up

As a student, you can follow the same steps as outlined above for the Equal Access Act but watch out for the following: When you speak with your principal be sure to state clearly that you want to set up a Christian club using the First Amendment Rights. This is also called a community club. If you are not crystal clear about that, the principal will probably give you paperwork for an Equal Access club.

For both types of clubs you need to do the following:

Get your legal documents ready

Before meeting with the principal, you need to make a copy of the legal information. Some are in the appendix others in the rest of the book.

✓ Milford Supreme Court Case (for First Amendment Clubs)
✓ Agencies which Support Faith-based Clubs
✓ Student Rights
✓ Guidance on Religious Expression in Public Schools
✓ Public Schools and Religious Communities
✓ Religion in the Public Schools: A Joint Statement of Current Law (highlight point 13)
✓ List of Organizations with more Information

1. Be sure to familiarize yourself with these documents so you can intelligently present your case. You might want to highlight certain paragraphs for the principal.

2. Take one or several friends along with you to the meeting, even if you do all the talking yourself. You can even bring the adult leader who will teach the class. This will show the principal interest. Plus, it provides moral support for you as your friend(s) can pray for you and back you up.

2. Highlight important portions of the documents. Put them in a pocket folder for the principal along with your name and contact info. Any principal who sees these documents will take you seriously and will refrain from saying no right away or try to come up with excuses. This will show them that you know your rights.

Research potential club materials

Meet with people such as:
✓ Youth Pastor
✓ Parents
✓ Senior Pastor
✓ Club members from other schools
Research online for youth group teachings:
✓ Youtube videos
✓ Books for youth group leaders
✓ Cru
✓ Young Lives
✓ One Voice

CHAPTER 39

SAMPLE HIGH SCHOOL PROPOSAL

Faircrest Christian Club

Faircrest High School
1111 Navarre Road
Navarre, OH 44660
Date

PERSON PRESENTING THE PROPOSAL:

Name: Jake Hurst

Email: xxxx

Address: xxxx

Phone: xxxx

NAME OF PROPOSED CLUB/ACTIVITY:

Faircrest Tribe

GENERAL DESCRIPTION OF PURPOSE OF PROPOSED CLUB/ ACTIVITY:

The Faircrest Tribe will be a fun and safe environment where students can learn about the Christian faith, make new friends, support each other, organize events and periodically participate in serving their community. We have snacks, games, music, teachings and discussions.

GOALS OF PROPOSED CLUB:

1. Strengthen moral and Christian values

2. Provide support for like-minded students

3. Open a fun, safe and upbuilding environment for students to discuss personal, family, and school topics

4. Cover subjects such as suicide prevention, bullying, life planning, and relationships. Reach out to all students with God's love.

5. Periodically invite speakers from the community

ACTIVITIES OR EVENTS STUDENTS WILL PARTICIPATE IN:

1. Weekly meetings

2. Possible additional gatherings

3. Possible community serving events

TYPE OF ROOM REQUESTED:

Classroom, library, or cafeteria

MEETING DAYS/TIMES:

Students will meet weekly during non-instructional time.

Thank you for your consideration.

CHAPTER 40

ORGANIZATIONS WHO CAN HELP

Cru High School Ministry

Helps pastors and students to set up a club. Here are some highlights of their work.

Share in the Vision. Cru helps you to identify your vision such as finding out how you would like to impact your schools and what needs of teenagers are most pressing on your heart. Then they help you share that vision.

Pray. They show you how to mobilize students to pray and to develop prayer partners, Their website has downloadable worksheets.:
Worksheets
Mobilizing Students to Pray[92]
Developing Prayer Partners[93]

Scout the Campus. You will learn how to scout the campus and find out who's who on campus.
Worksheets
Getting to Know your School[94]

---

[92] http://www.cruhighschool.com/resource/mobilizing-students-to-pray/
[93] http://www.cruhighschool.com/resource/developing-prayer-partners/
[94] http://www.cruhighschool.com/resource/getting-to-know-your-school/

Meet and Gather Students. They show you how to meet up with other student groups.
Worksheets
Meeting and Relating to Students[95]
Gathering Students[96]
Becoming an Insider[97]
Taking the Initiative[98]

Decode the Campus. Cru teaches you to find organic student groups.
Worksheets
Decode/Map the Campus[99]

Choose a Group to Reach. Identify which groups you want to reach and prioritize
Worksheets from Cru
Planning and Conducting an Outreach
Outreach Ideas[100]
How to Follow Up New Christian[101]
Faith Tracks Studies[102]

Youth for Christ

Youth for Christ has staff members who set up clubs in schools. They work closely with churches, parents, and faith-based organizations in the community.

Their website is a powerhouse of resources. You can download an entire curriculum for the semester. They have a new curriculum most years with both old and new downloadable on lessons such as *Inside my: anger, fear, sadness,* etc.

You will find not only curriculum, but you can find games like food,

---

[95] http://www.cruhighschool.com/resource/meeting-and-relating-to-students/
[96] http://www.cruhighschool.com/resource/gathering-students/
[97] http://www.cruhighschool.com/resource/becoming-an-insider/
[98] http://www.cruhighschool.com/resource/taking-the-initiative/
[99] http://www.cruhighschool.com/resource/mapping-your-campus/
[100] http://www.cruhighschool.com/resource-tags/outreach/
[101] http://www.cruhighschool.com/resource/how-to-follow-up-new-Christians/
[102] http://www.cruhighschool.com/resource/faith-track-Bible-studies/

water, or paint wars. They have curriculum modules on love, faith, community, etc. There are also modules and videos on building the club. The website has invaluable information for your choosing.

YFC also offers specific city life clubs and training manual[103] for leaders.

Be sure to look up campus life.[104]

Fellowship of Christian Athletes

FCA has made an enormous impact on our Nation. Have you ever wondered why so many professional athletes openly give God the credit? You don't see that from Hollywood or other fields. I believe that the Fellowship of Athletes has much to do with that.

This is the best way to reach out to athletes. If you are a youth pastor or a student who's into athletics you might want to go this route.

Team Huddles are the smallest and easiest clubs to set up. It encourages sports teams to live and compete within Christian principles.

FCA recommends two types of team Huddles:

1. Weekly Team Devotion: This usually takes place around practice times

2. Team Chapel: This is a game-day gathering for fellowship and spiritual uplifting.

FCA has information on Team Huddles[105] and devotionals to download.

Young Life

---

[103] http://www.yfc.net/resources/volunteer-in-training-manual-raising-indigenous-leaders-from-your-city-life

[104] http://www.yfc.net/campuslife/about/mission/

[105] http://www.fca.org/get-involved/huddles/team

Their clubs usually meet in the home of a student or at a community building. Therefore it doesn't have to be set up via the school and is usually taught by an adult Young Life coach. Young Life leaders network with and visit students during lunch, but the clubs are not typically set up as official school clubs.

Find out if your school has a Young Life Club[106] here: Contact the Young Life office near you

They offer two levels of involvement: The Club and the Campaigners.

Club
The club is open to anyone and is a place they say, "You'll yell, sing, watch wacky competitions and laugh" and of course "learn more about God and new ways of looking at life".

Campaigners
This is a more in-depth meeting discussing the Bible topics of interest to teens.

Many students attend both, the club and the campaigners. The club is about lots of fun and seeker friendly.

Young Life also offers clubs for middle schoolers called WyldLife[107]

Plus they offer a club for teenage mothers called Young*Lives*[108]

One Voice Student Mission

A Fairly New Organization Called One Voice Started In California About A Decade Ago and Has Amazing Results One Voice Student Missions[109] has been started by Brian Barcelona, a former high school student in California who felt the call to bring God to high schools throughout California and the US. They don't help set up a club but help to grow an existing one. Their model is a three legged stool:

---

[106] https://www.younglife.org/Locator/Pages/default.aspx

[107] https://www.younglife.org/ForEveryKid/WyldLife/Pages/default.aspx

[108] https://www.younglife.org/ForEveryKid/YoungLives/Pages/default.aspx

[109] http://onevoicestudentmissions.com

1. Work with established student clubs
2. Soak it in prayer
3. Work closely with local churches

Established Student Clubs

Typically, he works with the established Christian clubs at schools. He comes in as a dynamic speaker to help build the club. Brian Barcelona just wrote a brand-new book called the Jesus Club[110] which is full of amazing stories of what God is doing in high schools throughout California.

Prayer

Brian Barcelona listens closely to the Lord and obtains instructions from God through prayer. He knows he cannot do this by himself. God arranged for him and his wife, Marcella, to hook up with Lou Engle's national prayer movement, The Call. The strong emphasis on prayer is reflected in the name One Voice, meaning a body of believers praying together as one voice.

Local churches

One Voice student missions works closely with local churches and youth pastors. Their hope is to get students plugged in all the way. Churches adopt the Jesus club and support it in three ways:

1. Teaching: Providing teachers and or mentors for the club
2. Financial: Support: for food and materials
3. Prayer: Lifting up the club in prayer

---

[110] https://www.amazon.com/Jesus-Club-Incredible-Stories-Schools/dp/0800798198

CHAPTER 41

COMMUNICATING WITH ATHEISTS

Most high schools have gay-straight clubs, and many of those members are atheists. Being aware of potential opposition can prevent problems and help you stay clear of certain situations. Opposing views don't have to result in antagonism. It would be ideal for both the Christian club and the predominantly atheist gay-straight club to agree to disagree respectfully. This chapter will help to improve communication with atheists to foster better relations between the two.

Atheists frequently arrive at their conclusion after considerable research into religion. According to their verdict religion falls short on empirical science, their expectation, and even morals. Atheists beliefs are genuine, honest and intellectual. Many are well versed in certain scriptures. It's imperative to honor their belief and not to take every chance to try to change it without investing time and effort. It's better to offer mutual respect.

There is a reason why you believe in God and others don't. Most people make the mistake of approaching others with their own set of views, not bothering to try to get an idea of why people decide to doubt the existence of God. Since some of the very ardent atheist today are familiar with faith, it's important to find out what happened to them and prevent a repeat offense.

Faith and Facts

In many cases, atheists have had some form of belief earlier in life or were obligated to attend church. There is a reason for their vehement denial of God, or else they would be an agnostic, not caring either way.

Negative life experiences shape all of us. I'm not saying that all atheists have had bad experiences in their life. I suppose we would all like to have more proof and for God to show up at our front door and do miracles. It's true; I'd love to see God and not have to deal with faith. One atheist put it this way: "Showing me a picture of you and God in front of the Grand Canyon would be a step in the right direction." Here is another line I heard from an atheist, "Sure, get your God to show up during the meeting, that would convince me."

Those wishes are not that far-fetched as deep inside many of us would like to have clarity, and better yet, empirical proof. But God so honors our free will that He would never manipulate us into believing Him, so I suppose He doesn't want to be manipulated either to have to show up at the Grand Canyon.

The funny thing is that we're all on the same page. Even Thomas in the Bible said, "Show me, and I'll believe ." Jesus obliged and showed his scar to him, but Jesus was delighted by people who believed without solid proof. That's why it's called 'faith' not 'facts'. Believing is more mysterious than direct fact. He wants to communicate with our heart and spirit.

I've been at the other end of the spectrum, too. I grew up in Germany in a "Christian nation" where ironically almost no one believes in or knows God. In High School, I was not satisfied with science answering my questions about the origin of life. I asked everyone about God, especially if God is real, how I could find God, and where. No one could tell me, not even family and friends from my Lutheran church. I was told to live my life and forget about God. I am saying this to show that we all come from different directions and it is human nature to want proof.

The Dilemma

Christians in schools face the dilemma of living out biblical teachings without imposing them on non-believers. High school brings together people from different backgrounds, beliefs, and philosophies and they all have to get along. It's best to communicate sincerely with atheists and agnostics.

Regardless of people's viewpoint about the existence of God, the command to love our neighbor as ourselves places no restriction on who we are to love. One of the true marks of a Christian is love.

We are not qualified nor allowed to judge "Judge not, that ye be not judged." Matt. 7:1 This is a pivoting point when relating to atheists. Jesus was eager to meet with many people from different walks of lives and every time his love for them showed through Hais message. Only a sincere approach is effective. Fake smiles hiding behind a judgmental heart is a false expression of love and will do more harm than good.

Atheists Are Well Informed

Numerous atheist blogs and websites contain talking points against the Bible. I often notice that they focus on scriptures from the Old Testament and act as if the behavior of those people is endorsed by God just because the perpetrators believed in God. Other times scriptures are taken out of context. What we call good journalism today was practiced by God inspired biblical scribes who made sure the Bible tells true recollections of stories without taking out facts that make Christianity look bad. You can go through some of those stories and easily leave the bad stuff out, and yet no one throughout the centuries has tampered with the holy scriptures that way. In many other passages, God makes it clear that he does not approve of everything the prophets and patriarchs did. David is a case in point in the story of Bathsheba. God punished him severely for that sin. But can we truly say, that because David was a believer and yet committed horrible crimes, that we therefore do not believe in God? I never understood why some atheists equate God with ordinary fallible Christians. I think they believe that bad Christian behavior is proof the Christian doctrine doesn't work and therefore God doesn't exist. Or, maybe they are pointing fingers at what they call hypocrisy, but it is a mere excuse? I doubt that because I think they are smarter than that, but I also don't understand why many evaluate God by mere people's actions.

I have found that many atheists are interested in truth. Questions such as: Are you interested in truth? Can you evaluate the truth without worrying about what your friends will say? What about your pride and intellectualism? Science is continually finding evidence for biblical happenings. Lee Strobel's Hollywood film released in April 2016: "The Case for Christ" is full of that information and his book is written in an entertaining investigative style. It is worth knowing about those resources for those with an interest.

What About Morals?

Not believing in the existence of God does not necessarily mean those people believe that His laws are useless and ineffective. Many atheists adhere to a good moral code similar to the Ten Commandments. Acknowledging those morals from the get-go is paramount in establishing respect. Some atheists feel judged by Christians as having no morals simply because they don't refer to biblical morals. However, they just find other ways to redefine His commandments.

It's more likely that a friend listens to whatever you have to say than someone with whom you have no prior relationship. Jesus Christ did not try to convince Zacchaeus before He ate in his house. First, a relationship was formed, and by this relationship, Zacchaeus believed. High school provides numerous avenues to form relationships such as sports and other activities.

Should We Debate?

Very often we find ourselves being drawn into debates and arguments with atheists and most people approach this debate with the mind-set of using their knowledge of the Bible to convince others. However, atheists don't believe in the Bible, and God is not the author of confusion, but of peace. Hence the Holy Spirit would only do His work in peace. Our job is not always to lead people to Christ, but to share the message of love and to pray.

On the other hand, many atheists love to have a good conversation especially since they've already researched this subject. Be aware of their talking points as stated earlier: Atheist websites hone in on some scriptures which are difficult to understand in this day and age. They quote scriptures almost exclusively from the Old Testament which had to abide by strict laws. That's the very reason Jesus came - to do away with the law and change it over to grace. Jesus died for our sins so He could introduce grace and we no longer have to pay for our sins as in the Old Testament. Yes, some of those laws seem harsh, but that's the very reason God sacrificed his only son. Atheists primarily see a harsh God of the Old Testament and don't focus on the loving God of the New Testament. We need to be that light to show that the New

Testament takes precedence over the Old Testament.

The concept of sin is not meaningful to atheists. We know that if we don't adhere to the moral code of the scriptures, we sin. However, atheists don't believe in the Bible and therefore can't connect with the word sin. Many think the Bible contradicts itself and is just an arbitrary collection of stories and myths.[111]

Sharing Our Personal Journey

While a debate about science or intelligent design might not end well, our personal story and testimony cannot be as easily challenged. I have heard it wisely said, "no one wo has an experience is at the mercy of theory." Sharing how God touches us can create hunger in others for the same thing.

The scriptures say that through our testimony[112] people see God. Each one of us has a unique testimony from God to share with others. Let's stay faithful to that testimony and communicate it to the people God brings into our lives.

Do Scientists Believe in God?

We're often made to believe that scientists don't believe in God. However, there are notable exceptions:

"This most beautiful system of the sun, planets, and comets, could only proceed from the counsel and do minion of an intelligent and powerful Being."

Sir Isaac Newton

A more technical quote from Sir Isaac Newton[113] describes it this way:

---

[111] (2018). Witnessing to an Atheist.
Retrievable at:
http://www.firstgen.org/essays/evang1.htm
[112] Revelation 12.11
[113] Isaac Newton Theology, Prophecy, Science and Religion.
Retrievable at:
https://isaac-newton.org/general-scholium/

"He is Eternal and Infinite, Omnipotent and Omniscient; that is, his duration reaches from Eternity to Eternity; his presence from Infinity to Infinity; he governs all things, and knows all things that are or can be done. He is not Eternity and Infinity, but Eternal and Infinite; he is not Duration and Space, but he endures and is present. He endures forever, and is everywhere present; and, by existing always and everywhere, he constitutes Duration and Space. Since every particle of space is always, and every indivisible moment of duration is everywhere, certainly the Maker and Lord of all things cannot be never and nowhere."

Albert Einstein,[114] physicist and author of the Theory of Relativity, believed in God and even once admitted anger towards atheists. The book *Einstein: The Life and Times* states that the great scientist got angry at atheists for twisting his words to push their views. He was shocked why atheists keep on insisting that God does not exist and said:

"In view of such harmony in the cosmos which I, with my limited human mind, am able to recognize, there are yet people who say there is no God. But what really makes me angry is that they quote me for the support of such views."

In the book, *Einstein and the Poet. In Search of the Cosmic Man* by M. Berkowitz, the intelligent physicist described his sense of respect and amazement towards God's creations.

"'God' is a mystery. But a comprehensible mystery. I have nothing but awe when I observe the laws of nature. There are not laws without a lawgiver, but how does this lawgiver look? Certainly not like a man magnified."

Following is Albert Einstein's Interview with the Saturday Evening Post in 1929[115]

"The physicist, who was Jewish, said he was "enthralled by

---

[114] Calaprice, A. (2000).Page 215. The Expanded Quotable Einstein Princeton University.

[115] Mitchell, A. (2016). Albert Einstein 'absolutely not an atheist,' believed in God who brings 'harmony' in the universe.

the luminous figure of the Nazarene." When asked if he accepts the historical existence of Jesus Christ, Einstein replied, "Unquestionably! No one can read the Gospels without feeling the actual presence of Jesus. His personality pulsates in every word. No myth is filled with such life."

In *Einstein and Religion* by Max Jammer, Princeton University Press,[116] Einstein states:

"I'm not an atheist, and I don't think I can call myself a pantheist. We are in the position of a little child entering a huge library filled with books in many languages. The child knows someone must have written those books. It does not know how. It does not understand the languages in which they are written. The child dimly suspects a mysterious order in the arrangement of the books but doesn't know what it is. That, it seems to me, is the attitude of even the most intelligent human being toward God. We see the universe marvelously arranged and obeying certain laws but only dimly understand these laws. Our limited minds grasp the mysterious force that moves the constellations."

Einstein nevertheless admitted, despite his extraordinary intelligence, that the mystery of God is too vast for him to comprehend.

And one final quote from the scientist:

"Science without religion is lame, religion without science is blind."[117]

Seeker Friendly Christian Clubs

The primary focus on Christian clubs is for Christian students to get together in community. But it's also an opportunity to reach out to others. Like Christ, we can look for ways to make non-Christians feel welcome. Organizing extracurricular activities to draw students, both

---

[116] Jammer, M. (2002) Einstein and Religion, Princeton University Press
[117] Albert Einstein's Words on Spirituality and Religion.
Retrievable at:
http://archive.org/stream/AlbertEinsteinAndHisWorks/AlbertEinstein-WordsOnSpiritualityAndReligion.txt

Christians and non-Christians together, can form a basis for long-lasting relationships. Remember, a doctor who only opens his door to healthy patients is one who is not using his skills as designed. A Christian club that by its action, structure or behavior of its members closes the door on non-Christians is a tree that is not bearing fruit.

Ideas For Communicating with Atheists:

Even Christ himself, while talking to the woman at the well, did not immediately point out the fact that she was a hedonist or that he could offer her access to the water of life, the solutions to all her problems. First, he listened to her tell her side of the story, even though it was a lie.

The message of Christ is a message of love. It is a message whose very idea is mind- boggling. It is such good news that it is often not believed. We must demonstrate this message of love and not to merely try to convince people of its validity. The Holy Spirit ultimately knows how to reach people's heart. Living out the good examples of the Bible without necessarily preaching about it is more honoring. Showing in our actions that our life is happy and fulfilled believing in God speaks to people without preaching. It's difficult to reach atheists, and it might be better to focus on people who are open whether atheist, agnostic or seekers.

It's more natural to talk about our faith when it fits into a conversation and most genuine when presented as our testimony. However, it's paramount to stay brief and provide an opportunity for people to change the topic. If they're truly interested they'll keep the conversation going, if they don't and we keep going, our pushing can do more harm than good. We need to listen to people first and get to know them. People are not projects and we should express genuine interest in their lives. Their experiences carved their lives and made them who they are. It helps to pay close attention to what a person says because their statements reveal the strongholds that exist which also enables you to properly focus your prayers.

CHAPTER 42

STUDENT ASSEMBLIES

Academic entertainment in the form of student assemblies is popular at every school level from elementary through high Schools. Programs such as bully prevention, character education, music, cultural enrichment and social-emotional learning are offered by schools from kindergarten to high school.

Many Christian organizations and individuals offer such programs as well. The difference between school assemblies and Christian clubs is the Christian component. Because assemblies are attended by all students, any mention of God is prohibited as it would violate the Establishment Clause. In contrast, Christian clubs are voluntary and offered during non-instructional time and therefore are allowed to mention God freely.

So ,why are many assemblies offered by Christians if it's prohibited to talk about God? That answer is easier than you might think. Offering a suicide prevention program in high school shows students that you care and understand them. You can show that you're looking out for them and even have fun. After an assembly, people often have a sign-up sheet for students to meet in small groups to talk more about this. Students sign up voluntarily for an after-school club meeting and are informed that these meetings are also faith-based. So, this is a wonderful opportunity for students to get to know the presenter before signing up for a group. The school administration loves it because you teach valuable lessons their students need to hear without mentioning God.

The same option is available for elementary schools. In that case students will receive a flyer to take home which requires a parent's consent to attend further small groups after the assembly.

Few Christian organizations offer both student clubs and assemblies. However, you can find the Christian organizations which do assemblies and arrange a cooperative agreement. At the high school level, One Voice Student Missions is one of those exceptions who offer both. It's really an effective way to build Christian clubs.

Schoolshows.com is the largest nationwide directory of school assemblies which lists people/organizations offering them. You will not find a Christian category there, but viewing their performances online and researching further will give you clues.

CHAPTER 43

SEE YOU AT THE POLE

Does your school have a See You at the Pole event?

If yes, find out if the Christian club organizes it or whoever puts it together. Talk to the organizers, and if the school has no Christian club, you might want to connect with those Christians to start one.

If no, you might want to consider using this event as a launch for your Christian club.

Here's how See You at the Pole started...

A handful of teenagers in Burleson, Texas, met for a DiscipleNow weekend in early 1990. As they were praying, God touched their heart for their friends. On a Saturday night, they decided to drive to several schools and just pray. Without a specific plan and not knowing where exactly to go, they just went to each school's flagpole and prayed there.

Other youth leaders and prayer teams across Texas caught onto the vision, and they named their vision: "See You at the Pole". They talked about their vision to 20,0000 students in June 1990 at an arena in Texas. Only three months later, over 45,000 students prayed at the flagpoles of their schools in four different states.

At a youth pastor's conference in Colorado later that year many youth leaders talked about their students having a heart to pray after having heard what happened in Texas. In September the next year, one million students gathered around flag poles in their schools from East to West and North to South all over the nation.

To this day, the "See you at the pole" movement is alive and active with three million students attending and Christian clubs have sprung out of it.

Every year on the fourth Wednesday in September "See You at the Pole" events take place in schools across the nation. It's a prayer gathering, not a demonstration or rally. The students pray for their school, teachers, students and government.

As an informal gathering, students usually meet at 7 a.m. and join hands in prayer. Some of them may pray aloud and others may read short passages from the Bible or lead a song. Most groups start out small.

Over one million Christian students gathered for the 2016 "See you at the Pole" event nationwide. Sadie Robertson, the TV star on "Duck Dynasty," said in comments to The Christian Post[118] that the prayer event has "always meant something special to me. I think it's so cool that in our country so many teens still gather to pray at the pole each year. It is one of those things that keep our country wholesome, and reminds us all that it is in God whom we trust."

The mother of Rachel Joy Scott, who was shot at Columbine High School in 1999, also went back to the school to be with students in prayer.

Communities rally around our students and join in prayer for our schools, teachers, and families. It's an ideal platform to gather Christian students and follow up with launching or growing Christian clubs.

Those of you who are interested can find out more information on the See You at the Pole (SYATP) website.[119]

---

[118] Zaimov, S. (2016). 'See You at the Pole' 2016: Sadie Robertson Joins Millions of Teens Praying at Schools, Crying Out to God.
Retrievable at:
http://www.Christianpost.com/news/see-you-at-the-pole-2016-sadie-robertson-joins-millions-teenagers-praying-schools-crying-out-to-god-170170/
[119] http://syatp.com

You will find help in planning, promoting and organizing a SYATP prayer event. The site will also cover legal information on your rights. Of course, you have come this far in the book and most likely know your rights by now.

"Let us consider how to stimulate one another to love and good deeds, not forsaking assembling together, as is the habit of some, but encouraging one another; and all the more as you see the day drawing near." - Hebrews 10:24-25

CHAPTER 44

WHY NOT JUMP IN AND CONNECT

"And let us consider how to stir up one another to love and good works, not neglecting to meet together, as is the habit of some, but encouraging one another, and all the more as you see the Day drawing near."
Hebrews 10:24-25

If you are a teen, you know it can be easy to get used to your surroundings every day. After all, it's not uncommon to walk into your high school and hear vulgar language, gossip, and secular teaching. It's as if a spirit of confusion and antagonism to Christianity along with a fear of not being "politically right" hovers over these campuses. The administration often caves to the strong lobbyists of atheism - not out of conviction but merely to take the easier route and prevent trouble. This sad reality means that it is becoming harder for followers of Christ to rise above the crowd and stay close to God's truth.

At this age, peer pressure is on the rise, and unfortunately, many give into the 'pull' of the world around them. But Romans 12:2 says, "Do not be conformed to this world, but be transformed by the renewal of your mind, that by testing you may discern what the will of God, what is good and acceptable and perfect." We are called to resist the temptation to be like everyone else, and we are called to be a light in the darkness for the sake of Christ. It's a great responsibility with a greater reward.

The good news is that you don't have to do it alone. Starting or getting involved in a Christian club in your high school is a good way to get connected with a great community of believers who share your love for

Jesus and can sympathize with the struggles of being a Christian teen in a Godless world. Coming into contact with unsaved people every day can be discouraging, so you need friends and fellow Christians who will encourage you to keep trying and to keep shining, no matter the circumstances.

Proverbs 27:17 says, "Iron sharpens iron, and one man sharpens another." We were made for community. The best way to have that sense of community in the high school is to start a club or help grow an existing club. Your efforts will soon pay off in ways you could never imagine.

Christian clubs can be structured any way you want ranging from discussing certain topics from a biblical perspective, addressing current school issues, planning fun activities and whatever else people in your group are interested in.

There are so many fun, exciting activities that you can partake in as a group, whether it is during school or on your own time. Clubs don't just involve spiritual exercises like studying the Bible or praying; One of the most enjoyable aspects of the Christian life is simply hanging out with like-minded people.

Getting to know others is vital when you are focused on making a difference for Christ. Consider Acts 2:42: "And they devoted themselves to the apostles' teaching and the fellowship, to the breaking of bread and the prayers." The early church had a huge mission: To spread the love of Jesus. Yet, they did not overlook the importance of meeting together, eating together, and simply being in each other's presence. Before they could love the world around them, they had to learn to love each other.

Can you imagine how everyone reacted when they saw this awesome bond and community that these people shared? They were probably at least a little curious, and many came to know Christ because they observed believers simply being believers. Believe it or not, the same can happen in your high school.

So why not get involved? If nothing else, clubs can serve as a safe haven for those who are tired of all the negativity that society tries to impose upon them. Whether you start a club or just start to participate in one, there's no telling what kind of impact you can have. Never underestimate the mighty ways in which God can use you to build His Kingdom. And above all, remember the truth of 1 Timothy 4:12: "Let no one despise you for your youth, but set the believers an example in speech, in conduct, in love, in faith, in purity."

For we are his workmanship, created in Christ Jesus for good works, which God prepared beforehand, that we should walk in them.
Ephesians 2:10

PART FIVE

Organizations for Legal Help

CHAPTER 45

LIST OF ORGANIZATIONS WITH LEGAL INFORMATION

Advocates for Faith and Freedom [120]or call (888) 588-6888

Alliance Defending Freedom[121] or call (800) 835-5233

American Center for Law and Justice[122] or call (757) 226-2489

Christian Educators Association Intl.[123] or call (888) 798-1124

Center for Religious Expression[124] or call (901) 684-5485

Christian Legal Society [125]or call (703) 642-1070

Liberty Institute[126] or call (972) 941-4444

Liberty Counsel[127] or call (407) 875-1776

---

[120] http://www.crelaw.org
[121] Alliance Defending Freedom
[122] American Center for Law and Justice
[123] https://ceai.org
[124] Center for Religious Expression
[125] Christian Legal Society
[126] Liberty Institute
[127] Liberty Counsel

National Legal Foundation[128] or call (757) 463-6133

Rutherford Institute[129] or call (804) 978-3888

Pacific Justice Institute [130]or call (916) 857-6900

United States Justice Foundation [131]or call (760) 741-8086

More Organizations with Legal Information

List of organizations that can answer questions on religious expression in public schools. This list is from the US Dept. Of Ed Secretary Riley in 1998

Religious Action Center of Reform Judaism
Name: Rabbi David Saperstein
Address: 2027 Massachusetts Ave., NW, Washington, DC 20036
Phone: (202) 387-2800
Fax: (202) 667-9070
Website: http://www.rj.org/rac/

American Association of School Administrators
Name: Andrew Rotherham
Address: 1801 N. Moore St., Arlington, VA 22209
Phone: (703) 528-0700
Fax: (703) 528-2146
Website: http://www.aasa.org

American Jewish Congress
Name: Marc Stern
Address: 15 East 84th Street, New York, NY 10028
Phone: (212) 360-1545
Fax: (212) 861-7056

National PTA

---

[128] National Legal Foundation
[129] Rutherford Institute
[130] Pacific Justice Institute
[131] United States Justice Foundation

Name: Maribeth Oakes
Address: 1090 Vermont Ave., NW, Suite 1200, Washington, DC 20005
Phone: (202) 289-6790
Fax: (202) 289-6791
Website: http://www.pta.org

Christian Legal Society

Name: Steven McFarland
Address: 4208 Evergreen Lane, #222, Annandale, VA 22003
Phone: (703) 642-1070
Fax: (703) 642-1075
Website: http://www.clsnet.com

National Association of Evangelicals

Name: Forest Montgomery
Address: 1023 15th Street, NW #500, Washington, DC 20005
Phone: (202) 789-1011
Fax: (202) 842-0392
Website: http://www.nae.net

National School Boards Association

Name: Laurie Westley
Address: 1680 Duke Street, Alexandria, VA 22314
Phone: (703) 838-6703
Fax: (703) 548-5613
Web site: http://www.nsba.org

Freedom Forum

Name: Charles Haynes
Address: 1101 Wilson Blvd, Arlington, VA 22209
Phone: (703) 528-0800
Fax: (703) 284-2879
Website: http://www.freedomforum.org

CHAPTER 46

RELIGIOUS FREEDOM DAY

January 16th is Religious Freedom Day, and each President annually calls on people to observe this day through appropriate events and activities in homes, schools, and places of worship. This is a perfect opportunity to launch or grow Christian clubs by offering a special invitation to students.

You will find more information here:
http://religiousfreedomday.com

The Guidebook on Religious Freedom Day can be found on the front page of that website to download and print. Feel free to give it to teachers, principals, parents, and students. It contains information about our legal rights in a brief handout.

The Religious Freedom Day is based on Christian rights highlighted throughout this book. Each new term, the President of the United States reemphasizes the stand on the faith of the United States of America.

National Day of Prayer

2017 Proclamation by President Trump

"We come together on our National Day of Prayer as one Nation, under God, to show gratitude for our many blessings, to give thanks for His providence, and to ask for His continued wisdom, strength, and protection as we chart a course for the future."

1994 Proclamation by President Clinton

"Religious freedom helps to give America's people a character independent of their government, fostering the formation of individual codes of ethics, without which a democracy cannot survive."

1999 Proclamation by President Clinton

"Americans are a deeply religious people, and our right to worship as we choose, to follow our own personal beliefs, is the source of much of our Nation's strength."

2002 Proclamation by President Bush

"Religious freedom is a cornerstone of our Republic, a core principle of our Constitution, and a fundamental human right."

2013 Proclamation by President Obama

"As we observe Religious Freedom Day, let us remember the legacy of faith and independence we have inherited, and let us honor it by forever upholding our right to exercise our beliefs free from prejudice or persecution."

Part Six

High School Documents

CHAPTER 47

STUDENT BILL OF RIGHTS

The Right to Meet with Other Christian Students.

Students have the freedom to meet at school and form clubs for the purpose of discussing Christian issues.

The Right to Pray on Campus.

Students may pray alone or with others so long as it does not disrupt school activities or is not forced upon others.

Right to Identify Your Christian Beliefs Through Pins, Signs, Symbols, And Messages on Clothing.

You may make such statements as long as they are not vulgar or indecent.

The Right to Talk About Your Christian Beliefs on Campus.

The Free Speech Clause of the First Amendment allows you to freely express your belief in God.

The Right to Distribute Christian Literature on Campus.

Distributing religious literature at school may not be restricted just because it's Christian material. Faith-based literature from Bible clubs follows the same distribution policy as other clubs do.

The Right to Carry or Study Your Bible on Campus.

The Supreme Court has said that only state-directed Bible reading is unconstitutional.

The Right to Do Research Papers, Speeches, and Creative Projects with Religious Themes.

Students can freely express there believe in God in papers, Homework, creative projects or any other assignment. The Free Speech Clause of the First Amendment guarantees that right.

The Right to Be Exempt.

Students may be exempt from activities and class content that contradict their religious beliefs.

The Right to Celebrate or Study Christian Holidays on Campus.

Music, art, literature, and drama that have Christian themes are permitted as part of the curriculum for school activities if presented in an objective manner as a traditional part of the cultural and Christian heritage of the particular holiday.

The Right to Meet with School Officials.

The First Amendment to the Constitution forbids Congress to make any law that would not respect the right of the people to petition the government (school officials).

The Student Bill of Rights[132] applies to all schools including elementary schools. It's a statement for students based on the First Amendment's Free Speech and Free Excercise Rights.

Would you like a clean copy to take to meetings?
Go to: http://partnerwithschools.org/resources.html

---

[132] Brinkley J.W, Roever Communicatons. (1990) (Adapted)

CHAPTER 48

AGENCIES SUPPORTING FAITH-BASED PROGRAMS

Supreme Court

Supreme Court Verdict States: Religious Clubs Can Meet at Public Schools.[133]

"The Supreme Court ruled in favor of a voluntary Christian club which meets during non-instructional time and inside the school facilities. The majority found that excluding the club was unconstitutional discrimination based on the club's views. Letting the meeting take place would not be an unconstitutional government endorsement of religion, the court ruled."

United States Supreme Court
Good News Club et al. v. Milford Central School, (2001)

NEA

The National Education Association Is Pulling in Faith-Based Organizations to Improve Student Learning in Their Priority Schools Campaign.

---

[133] Good News Club et al. v Milford Central School, 533 U.S. 98 (2001)
Retrievable at:
http://caselaw.findlaw.com/us-supreme-court/533/98.html

Executive Summary: Strategy #5:[134]

"Building collaborations with community partners: Pulling in strategic partners and developing community by-in with colleges, social service agencies, community groups, faith-based organizations, local leaders, public officials, and businesses - to improve student learning and other outcomes."

Department Of Education

Promotes Student Achievement by Connecting Schools with Faith-Based Organizations:[135]

"The mission of the Center for Faith-based and Neighborhood Partnerships at the U.S. Department of Education is to promote student achievement by connecting schools and community-based organizations, both secular and faith-based."

The White House Office Of Faith-Based Partnerships

States That Faith and Community Groups are Critical Partners In Expanding Community Involvement:[136]

"Education is a critical pathway to success for individuals and families. Partnerships between schools and faith-based and community organizations can help to achieve this goal of educational success for all students. That is why the Center for Faith-Based and Neighborhood Partnerships at the Department of Education works to promote student

---

[134] Anne T. Henderson, Senior Consultant to the Annenberg Institute for School Reform, and co-author of A New Wave of Evidence: The Impact of School, Family, and Community Connections on Student Achievement and Beyond the Bake Sale: The Essential Guide to Family-School-Community Partnerships 2.0. National Education Association (NEA) 2011
Retrievable at:
http://www.nea.org/assets/docs/Family-School-Community-Partnerships-2.0.pdf
[135] Faith-based and Neighborhood Partnerships.
Retrievable at:
http://sites.ed.gov/fbnp/
[136] President Obama, (2010). PARTNERSHIPS for the COMMON GOOD.
Retrievable at:
https://obamawhitehouse.archives.gov/sites/default/files/faithbasedtoolkit.pdf

achievement and build a culture of educational excellence within communities across the country."

"The White House Office of Faith-based and Neighborhood Partnerships works to build bridges between the federal government and nonprofit organizations, both secular and faith-based, to better serve Americans in need. The Office advances this work through Centers in various Federal agencies."

The NEA Foundation

States That Successful School Districts Have Relied On Faith-Based Institutions:[137]

"Successful union and district collaborations have included creation of partnerships with community-based organizations, faith-based institutions, health and mental health agencies, and city or community-based agencies focused on developing comprehensive solutions for the complex challenges of educating all students."

NEA Today

Encourages Schools to Develop Meaningful Partnerships with Faith Organizations:[138]

"Local Partnerships to Transform Priority Schools. Partnerships between priority schools and their communities help students succeed—in school and in life."

"While some local associations and school districts are in the beginning phases of developing meaningful partnerships with local businesses, civic, faith and social organizations, and community coalitions, several priority schools are already seeing the benefits these partnerships can have for their students."

---

[137] The NEA Foundation Report (2012, April). Expanding Learning Opportunities to Close The Achievement Gaps: Lessons from Union-District Collaborations.
Retrievable at:
http://www.neafoundation.org/content/assets/2012/04/elo-final-2.pdf
[138] Buffenbarger, A. (2011). Faith-based and Neighborhood Partnerships.
Retrievable at:
http://www.nea.org/tools/48684.htm

ACLU

States That: "Student-Organized Bible Clubs[139] **Are Ok as Long as Three Conditions Are Met:**

(1) the activity must take place during non-school hours;

(2) school officials can't be involved in organizing or running the club, and

(3) the school must make its facilities available to all student groups on an equal basis."

Would you like a clean copy to take to meetings?
Go to: http://partnerwithschools.org/resources.html

---

[139] (2018)YOUR RIGHT TO RELIGIOUS FREEDOM.
Retrievable at:
https://www.aclu.org/other/your-right-religious-freedom

CHAPTER 49

ACLU STANDING UP FOR CHRISTIANS

The American Civil Liberties Union of Tennessee has offered to defend a local Cannon County boy who was recently told that he could not read a Bible during an after-school program.

The ACLU of Tennessee has sent a letter to the Cannon County REACH after-school program on behalf of the boy, who attends an elementary school. The Cannon County. The Staff of the REACH program reportedly told the boy that he could not read the Bible during a free-reading period. The staff then tried to take the Bible, telling him the after-school program could lose its state funds if they allowed him to continue reading it.

In the letter sent to the REACH program, the ACLU requests that the after-school program train its employees on religious freedom rights while not imposing religion on the students. It also requests that the after-school program allow the student to continue reading his Bible during the free-reading period or any other student activity time.

"Tennessee public school students cannot be denied the right to engage in religious activities during student activity times, recess and other free time, provided they do not cause a disruption or interfere with the education of other students. Reading the Bible, or any other religious text, during a free-read period would fall within these protected freedoms," the letter states.

Hedy Weinberg, executive director for the ACLU's Tennessee branch, also said in a statement that the goal of their letter is to clarify how constitutionally-guaranteed religious freedoms work.

by K. Weber, Christian Post Report April 2, 2014

Would you like a clean copy to take to meetings?
Go to: http://partnerwithschools.org/resources.html

CHAPTER 50

DISCLAIMER LANGUAGE

Following paragraph can be added as small print to flyers or any printed material. It can also be stated after a public announcement of an event.

The United States Constitution requires schools to respect the right of all external organizations to distribute flyers to students at school if the school permits any such organization to distribute flyers. Accordingly, the school cannot discriminate among groups wishing to distribute flyers at school and does not endorse the content of any flyer distributed at school. The school encourages parents to assist their students in making choices appropriate for them. This is not an activity of the school or the school district.

Would you like a clean copy to take to meetings?
Go to: http://partnerwithschools.org/resources.html

PART SEVEN

Federal Guidelines On Faith In Public Schools

CHAPTER 51

LEGAL GUIDELINES REGARDING THE EQUAL ACCESS ACT

U.S. DEPARTMENT OF EDUCATION

LEGAL GUIDELINES REGARDING THE EQUAL ACCESS ACT AND THE RECOGNITION OF STUDENT-LED NONCURRICULAR GROUPS

The Equal Access Act ensures that noncurricular student groups are afforded the same access to public secondary school facilities as other, similarly situated student groups. Based on decisions of the U.S. Supreme Court and other federal courts interpreting the Act, the U.S. Department of Education's Office of the General Counsel provides the following guidance.

1. General Scope

The Act applies to: (1) any public secondary school (2) that receives federal funds (3) and creates a limited open forum by allowing one or more noncurricular student groups to meet on its premises (4) during noninstructional time. Schools meeting these criteria are forbidden to prevent access or deny fair opportunity to students who wish to hold meetings on school grounds.

The Act does not mention specific types of student groups to which equal-access rights apply. It instead broadly provides that schools allowing at least one "noncurriculum related student group" may not deny comparable access to any other student group because of the "religious, political, philosophical, or other content of the speech at [the group's] meetings." The Act therefore prohibits schools from banning student-led noncurricular groups because of the content of the speech at the groups' meetings.

The Act identifies narrow exceptions; however, schools may not ban or suppress the speech of student groups based on a "desire to avoid the discomfort and unpleasantness that always accompany an unpopular viewpoint."

2. Legal Principles and Obligations

When framing policies regarding equal access, schools are advised to consider the following:

- If a federally funded public secondary school allows at least one noncurriculum-related student group to meet on school premises during noninstructional time, it has created a "limited open forum" that triggers the Act's protections. In that case, the school may not deny the same access for similarly situated clubs on the basis of the content of the clubs' speech.
- "Access" refers not only to physical meeting spaces on school premises, but also to recognition and privileges afforded to other groups at the school, including, for example, the right to announce club meetings in the school newspaper, on bulletin boards, or over the public-address system. Noninstructional time is "time set aside by the school before actual classroom instruction begins or after actual instruction ends," and covers student meetings that take place before or after school as well as those occurring during lunch, "activity periods," and other noninstructional periods during the school day.
- The Supreme Court defines a curriculum-related student group as one that "directly relates" to the body of courses offered at a school. A student group directly relates to a school's curriculum "if the subject matter of the group is actually taught, or will soon be taught, in a regularly offered course; if the subject matter of the group concerns the body of courses as a whole; if participation in the group is required for a particular course; or if participation in the group results in academic credit." According to the Supreme Court, for example, a "French club would directly relate to the curriculum if a school taught French in a regularly offered course or planned to teach the subject in the

near future."

- Schools retain the right to exclude groups that are directed, conducted, controlled, or regularly attended by nonschool persons.
- Noncurricular student groups may have faculty sponsors without compromising the requirement that they are student-initiated. "The assignment of a teacher, administrator, or other school employee to a meeting for custodial purposes does not constitute sponsorship of the meeting."
- Schools retain authority to ban unlawful groups, maintain discipline and order on school premises, protect the well-being of students and faculty, assure that students' attendance at meetings is voluntary, and restrict groups that materially and substantially interfere with the orderly conduct of educational activities. But the Act does not permit schools to ban groups or suppress student speech based on unpopularity of the message or on unfounded fears that the group may incite violence or disruption. Where the material and substantial interference is caused not by the group itself but by those who oppose the group's formation or message, the disruption will not justify suppressing the group.

3. Issues to Consider When Applying the Act

- Viewing Access as an Endorsement of a Student Group or its Message: A school may not discriminate against a student group on the basis that allowing access would constitute an endorsement of the group. The U.S. Supreme Court has specifically recognized that public "schools do not endorse everything they fail to censor," because secondary school students are generally capable of understanding that schools do not endorse or support speech that an institution merely permits on a nondiscriminatory basis. Thus, granting access on a nondiscriminatory basis does not constitute a school's endorsement of a group's activities, and avoiding the appearance of endorsement does not, therefore, justify denying the group equal access.
- Defining the Meaning of "Curriculum Related" Too Broadly: If a school has not created a limited open forum (i.e., the only student groups are curricular), the Act does not require the

school to grant a request to allow a noncurricular group to meet. The meaning of "curriculum related" cannot, however, be broadened in ways that would render the Act meaningless. For example, a school cannot evade the Act by declaring that all existing student clubs are curricular, and invoking some broad, vague educational goals that they all serve, while labeling as noncurricular any student groups that it wishes to exclude. What matters are the groups' actual relationships to the curriculum and the school's actual practices in granting access.

- Banning All Noncurricular Groups: A school could close a limited open forum by banning all noncurricular groups, thereby avoiding any obligations under the Act. But successfully closing a previously open forum will often prove difficult: In an Equal Access Act challenge, a written policy banning noncurricular clubs is insufficient and a court will scrutinize a school's actual practices to ensure each remaining club is genuinely curricular.

- Invoking Moral Reasons or Censorship of Explicit Content: The Act guarantees schools' right "to protect the well-being of students and faculty." And the U.S. Supreme Court has recognized that public schools may restrict students' access to and expression of obscene or sexually explicit material to protect students. But the Act does not permit schools to ban a group based on school officials' general moral disapproval or on assumptions about the content of speech at group meetings. A school would, for example, violate the Act by excluding a group based on the fact that it addresses issues of interest to members of a minority faith or to lesbian, gay, bisexual and transgender (LGBT) students.

- Viewing Student Groups as Controlled or Directed by Nonschool Persons: Schools may uniformly deny access to groups that are controlled, directed, or regularly attended by nonschool persons. But schools may not exclude certain student groups merely because of national affiliations, while providing access to other groups with similar affiliations. For instance, if a school recognizes a service club or honor society such as Beta Club or Key Club that shares its name with a national organization, the school cannot deny access to a gay-straight alliance merely because it shares a name with a national organization

- Imposing Special Requirements on Some Student Groups: The

Act requires the school to treat each group like other, similarly situated groups, and prohibits imposing additional requirements on some student-run groups that are not imposed on all others. A school would violate the Act by, for example, requiring a gay-straight alliance to change its name, requiring it to have a faculty adviser when faculty advisers are not generally required for all other groups, or imposing different requirements for the group's posters, leaflets, and announcements than the school places on other groups' promotional materials.

Would you like a clean copy to take to meetings?
Go to: http://partnerwithschools.org/resources.html

CHAPTER 52

THE EQUAL ACCESS ACT PUBLIC LAW

**The Equal Access Act
(Title VIII of Public Law 98-377)**

**Denial of Equal Access Prohibited
Sec. 802.**

(a) It shall be unlawful for any public secondary school which receives Federal financial assistance and which has a limited open forum to deny equal access or a fair opportunity to, or discriminate against, any students who wish to conduct a meeting within that limited open forum on the basis of the religious, political, philosophical, or other content of the speech at such meetings.

(b) A public secondary school has a limited open forum whenever such school grants an offering to or opportunity for one or more non-curriculum related student groups to meet on school premises during non-instructional time.

(c) Schools shall be deemed to offer a fair opportunity to students who wish to conduct a meeting within its limited open forum if such school uniformly provides that --

> (1) the meeting is voluntary and student-initiated;
>
> (2) there is no sponsorship of the meeting by the school, the government, or its agents or employees;

(3) employees or agents of the school or government are present at religious meetings only in a nonparticipatory capacity;

(4) the meeting does not materially and substantially interfere with the orderly conduct of educational activities within the school; and

(5) nonschool persons may not direct, conduct, control, or regularly attend activities of student groups.

(d) Nothing in this title shall be construed to authorize the United States or any State or political subdivision thereof --

(1) to influence the form or content of any prayer or other religious

(2) to require any person to participate in prayer or other religious

(3) to expend public funds beyond the incidental cost of providing the space for student-initiated meetings;

(4) to compel any school agent or employee to attend a school meeting if the content of the speech at the meeting is contrary to the beliefs of the agent or employee;

(5) to sanction meetings that are otherwise unlawful;

(6) to limit the rights of groups of students which are not of a specified numerical size; or

(7) to abridge the constitutional rights of any person.

(e) Notwithstanding the availability of any other remedy under the Constitution or the laws of the United States, nothing in this title shall be construed to authorize the United States to deny or withhold Federal financial assistance to any school.

(f) Nothing in this title shall be construed to limit the authority of the school, its agents or employees, to maintain order and discipline on school premises, to protect the well-being of students and faculty, and to assure that attendance of students at meetings is voluntary.

Definitions
Sec. 803.

As used in this title --

(1) The term "secondary school" means a public school which provides secondary education as determined by State law.

(2) The term "sponsorship" includes the act of promoting, leading, or participating in a meeting. The assignment of a teacher, administrator, or other school employee to a meeting for custodial purposes does not constitute sponsorship of the meeting.

(3) The term "meeting" includes those activities of student groups which are permitted under a school's limited open forum and are not directly related to the school curriculum.

(4) The term "noninstructional time" means time set aside by the school before actual classroom instruction begins or after actual classroom instruction ends.

Severability
Sec. 804.

If any provision of this title or the application thereof to any person or circumstances is judicially determined to be invalid, the provisions of the remainder of the title and the application to other persons or circumstances shall not be affected thereby.

Construction
Sec. 805.

The provisions of this title shall supersede all other provisions of Federal law that are inconsistent with the provisions of this title.

Would you like a clean copy to take to meetings?
Go to: http://partnerwithschools.org/resources.html

PART EIGHT

Appendix

CHAPTER 53

RELIGION IN THE PUBLIC SCHOOLS: A JOINT STATEMENT

JOINT STATEMENT OF CURRENT LAW ON RELIGION IN THE PUBLIC SCHOOLS

Religion In The Public Schools:
A Joint Statement Of Current Law

The Constitution permits much private religious activity in and about the public schools. Unfortunately, this aspect of constitutional law is not as well known as it should be. Some say that the Supreme Court has declared the public schools "religion-free zones" or that the law is so murky that school officials cannot know what is legally permissible. The former claim is simply wrong. And as to the latter, while there are some difficult issues, much has been settled. It is also unfortunately true that public school officials, due to their busy schedules, may not be as fully aware of this body of law as they could be. As a result, in some school districts some of these rights are not being observed.

The organizations whose names appear below span the ideological, religious and political spectrum. They nevertheless share a commitment both to the freedom of religious practice and to the separation of church and state such freedom requires. In that spirit, we offer this statement of consensus on current law as an aid to parents, educators and students.

Many of the organizations listed below are actively involved in litigation about religion in the schools. On some of the issues discussed in this summary, some of the organizations have urged the courts to reach positions different than they did. Though there are signatories on both sides which have and will press for different constitutional treatments of some of the topics discussed below, they all agree that the following is an accurate statement of what the law currently is.

Student Prayers

1. Students have the right to pray individually or in groups or to discuss their religious views with their peers so long as they are not disruptive. Because the Establishment Clause does not apply to purely private speech, students enjoy the right to read their Bibles or other scriptures, say grace before meals, pray before tests, and discuss religion with other willing student listeners. In the classroom students have the right to pray quietly except when required to be actively engaged in school activities (e.g., students may not decide to pray just as a teacher calls on them). In informal settings, such as the cafeteria or in the halls, students may pray either audibly or silently, subject to the same rules of order as apply to other speech in these locations. However, the right to engage in voluntary prayer does not include, for example, the right to have a captive audience listen or to compel other students to participate.

Graduation Prayer and Baccalaureates

2. School officials may not mandate or organize prayer at graduation, nor may they organize a religious baccalaureate ceremony. If the school generally rents out its facilities to private groups, it must rent them out on the same terms, and on a first- come first-served basis, to organizers of privately sponsored religious baccalaureate services, provided that the school does not extend preferential treatment to the baccalaureate ceremony and the school disclaims official endorsement of the program.

3. The courts have reached conflicting conclusions under the federal Constitution on student-initiated prayer at graduation. Until the issue is authoritatively resolved, schools should ask their lawyers what rules apply in their area.

Official Participation or Encouragement of Religious Activity

4. Teachers and school administrators, when acting in those capacities, are representatives of the state, and, in those capacities, are themselves prohibited from encouraging or soliciting student religious or anti-religious activity. Similarly, when acting in their official capacities, teachers may not engage in religious activities with their students. However, teachers may engage in private religious activity in faculty lounges.

Teaching About Religion

5. Students may be taught about religion, but public schools may not teach religion. As the U.S. Supreme Court has repeatedly said, "[i]t might well be said that one's education is not complete without a study of comparative religion, or the history of religion and its relationship to the advancement of civilization." It would be difficult to teach art, music, literature and most social studies without considering religious influences.

The history of religion, comparative religion, the Bible (or other scripture)-as-literature (either as a separate course or within some other existing course), are all permissible public school subjects. It is both permissible and desirable to teach objectively about the role of religion in the history of the United States and other countries. One can teach that the Pilgrims came to this country with a particular religious vision, that Catholics and others have been subject to persecution or that many of those participating in the abolitionist, women's suffrage and civil rights movements had religious motivations.

6. These same rules apply to the recurring controversy surrounding theories of evolution. Schools may teach about explanations of life on earth, including religious ones (such as "creationism"), in comparative religion or social studies classes. In science class, however, they may present only genuinely scientific critiques of, or evidence for, any explanation of life on earth, but not religious critiques (beliefs unverifiable by scientific methodology). Schools may not refuse to teach evolutionary theory in order to avoid giving offense to religion nor may they circumvent these rules by labeling as science an article of religious faith. Public schools must not teach as scientific fact or theory any religious doctrine, including "creationism," although any genuinely scientific evidence for or against any explanation of life may be taught.

Just as they may neither advance nor inhibit any religious doctrine, teachers should not ridicule, for example, a student's religious explanation for life on earth.

Student Assignments and Religion

7. Students may express their religious beliefs in the form of reports, homework and artwork, and such expressions are constitutionally protected. Teachers may not reject or correct such submissions simply because they include a religious symbol or address religious themes. Likewise, teachers may not require students to modify, include or excise religious views in their assignments, if germane. These assignments should be judged by ordinary academic standards of substance, relevance, appearance and grammar.

8. Somewhat more problematic from a legal point of view are other public expressions of religious views in the classroom. Unfortunately for school officials, there are traps on either side of this issue, and it is possible that litigation will result no matter what course is taken. It is easier to describe the settled cases than to state clear rules of law. Schools must carefully steer between the claims of student speakers who assert a right to express themselves on religious subjects and the asserted rights of student listeners to be free of unwelcome religious persuasion in a public school classroom.

a. Religious or anti-religious remarks made in the ordinary course of classroom discussion or student presentations are permissible and constitute a protected right. If in a sex education class a student remarks that abortion should be illegal because God has prohibited it, a teacher should not silence the remark, ridicule it, rule it out of bounds or endorse it, any more than a teacher may silence a student's religiously-based comment in favor of choice.

b. If a class assignment calls for an oral presentation on a subject of the student's choosing, and, for example, the student responds by conducting a religious service, the school has the right -- as well as the duty -- to prevent itself from being used as a church. Other students are not voluntarily in attendance and cannot be forced to become an unwilling congregation.

c. Teachers may rule out-of-order religious remarks that are irrelevant to the subject at hand. In a discussion of Hamlet's sanity, for example, a student may not interject views on creationism.

Distribution of Religious Literature

9. Students have the right to distribute religious literature to their schoolmates, subject to those reasonable time, place, and manner or other constitutionally- acceptable restrictions imposed on the distribution of all non-school literature. Thus, a school may confine distribution of all literature to a particular table at particular times. It may not single out religious literature for burdensome regulation.

10. Outsiders may not be given access to the classroom to distribute religious or anti-religious literature. No court has yet considered whether, if all other community groups are permitted to distribute literature in common areas of public schools, religious groups must be allowed to do so on equal terms subject to reasonable time, place and manner restrictions.

"See You at the Pole"

11. Student participation in before- or after-school events, such as "see you at the pole," is permissible. School officials, acting in an official capacity, may neither discourage nor encourage participation in such an event.

Religious Persuasion Versus Religious Harassment

12. Students have the right to speak to, and attempt to persuade, their peers about religious topics just as they do with regard to political topics. But school officials should intercede to stop student religious speech if it turns into religious harassment aimed at a student or a small group of students. While it is constitutionally permissible for a student to approach another and issue an invitation to attend church, repeated invitations in the face of a request to stop constitute harassment. Where this line is to be drawn in particular cases will depend on the age of the students and other circumstances.

Equal Access Act

13. Student religious clubs in secondary schools must be permitted to meet and to have equal access to campus media to announce their meetings, if a school receives federal funds and permits any student non-curricular club to meet during non-instructional time. This is the command of the Equal Access Act. A non-curricular club is any club not related directly to a subject taught or soon-to-be taught in the school. Although schools have the right to ban all non-curriculum clubs, they may not dodge the law's requirement by the expedient of declaring all clubs curriculum-related. On the other hand, teachers may not actively participate in club activities and "non-school persons" may not control or regularly attend club meeting.

The Act's constitutionality has been upheld by the Supreme Court, rejecting claims that the Act violates the Establishment Clause. The Act's requirements are described in more detail in The Equal Access Act and the Public Schools: Questions and Answers on the Equal Access Act*, a pamphlet published by a broad spectrum of religious and civil liberties groups.

Religious Holidays

14. Generally, public schools may teach about religious holidays, and may celebrate the secular aspects of the holiday and objectively teach about their religious aspects. They may not observe the holidays as religious events. Schools should generally excuse students who do not wish to participate in holiday events. Those interested in further details should see Religious Holidays in the Public Schools: Questions and Answers*, a pamphlet published by a broad spectrum of religious and civil liberties groups.

Excusal From Religiously-Objectionable Lessons

15. Schools enjoy substantial discretion to excuse individual students from lessons which are objectionable to that student or to his or her parent on the basis of religion. Schools can exercise that authority in ways which would defuse many conflicts over curriculum content. If it is proved that particular lessons substantially burden a student's free exercise of religion and if the school cannot prove a compelling interest in requiring attendance the school would be legally required to excuse

the student.

Teaching Values

16. Schools may teach civic virtues, including honesty, good citizenship, sportsmanship, courage, respect for the rights and freedoms of others, respect for persons and their property, civility, the dual virtues of moral conviction and tolerance and hard work. Subject to whatever rights of excusal exist (see #15 above) under the federal Constitution and state law, schools may teach sexual abstinence and contraception; whether and how schools teach these sensitive subjects is a matter of educational policy. However, these may not be taught as religious tenets. The mere fact that most, if not all, religions also teach these values does not make it unlawful to teach them.

Student Garb

17. Religious messages on T-shirts and the like may not be singled out for suppression. Students may wear religious attire, such as yarmulkes and head scarves, and they may not be forced to wear gym clothes that they regard, on religious grounds, as immodest.

Released Time

18. Schools have the discretion to dismiss students to off-premises religious instruction, provided that schools do not encourage or discourage participation or penalize those who do not attend. 20. Schools may not allow religious instruction by outsiders on premises during the school day.

Appendix

Organizational Signers of "Religion in the Public Schools: A Joint Statement of Current Law"
American Civil Liberties Union
American Ethical Union
American Humanist Association
American Jewish Committee
American Jewish Congress
American Muslim Council

Americans for Religious Liberty
Americans United for Seperation of Church and State
Anti-Defamation League
Baptist Joint Committee
B'nai B'rith
Christian Legal Society
Christian Science Church
Church of Scientology International
Evangelical Lutheran Church in America,
Lutheran Office for Governmental Affairs
Federation of Reconstructionist Congregations and Havurot
Friends Committee on National Legislation
General Conference of Seventh-day Adventists
Guru Gobind Singh Foundation
Interfaith Alliance
Interfaith Impact for Justice and Peace
National Association of Evangelicals
National Council of Churches
National Council of Jewish Women
National Jewish Community Relations Advisory Council (NJCRAC)
National Ministries, American Baptist Churches, USA
National Sikh Center
North American Council for Muslim Women
People for the American Way
Presbyterian Church (USA)
Reorganized Church of Jesus Christ of Latter Day Saints
Union of American Hebrew Congregations
Unitarian Universalist Association of Congregations
United Church of Christ, Office for Church in Society

Would you like a clean copy to take to meetings?
Go to: http://partnerwithschools.org/resources.html

CHAPTER 54

ADDITIONAL RESOURCES

If you would like additional information, you can find it on our website at: Partner with Schools: http://partnerwithschools.org/resources.html[140]

Documents available:

Federal Government Information

Guidance On Religious Expression In Public Schools
A Parent's Guide To Religion In The Public Schools
Guidance On Constitutionally Protected Prayer
Proclamation by U.S. Presidents on the National Day of Prayer

K-12 Schools

Student Bill of Rights
Disclaimer Language

Elementary School Documents

Sample Permission Form for Elementary Schools
Sample Leader Application
Safety Policy and Background Check
Supreme Court Allows Christian Clubs

High School Documents

Agencies Supporting Faith-Based Programs
ACLU Standing up for Christians

---

[140] https://www.facebook.com/partnerwithschools/

Partner with Schools provides coaching for individuals and churches. Ingrid DeDecker speaks at conferences and in churches:
Connect@partnerwithschools.org

For questions and to connect with the author, feel free to send an email to:
dedecker@partnerwithschools.org

or visit our FB group:
https://www.facebook.com/partnerwithschools/

If this book was helpful to you please go to the book's Amazon page and leave a quick review. https://www.amazon.com/BRING-LIGHT-SCHOOL-Christian-Students-ebook/dp/B07C52WL3S/ref=tmm_kin_swatch_0?_encoding=UTF8&qid=1523571772&sr=1-1-spell
Right underneath the title you'll find the review option. The more reviews, the more Amazon will market the book and the more people will bring The Light to Schools.

This book is also enabled to loan out to friends. On your own Amazon page you can go to Account and then Your Content and find the title of the book which will have a loan option. After two weeks it will automatically return to you.